REGIS COLLEGE LIBRARY
100 Wellesley Street West
Toronto, Ontario
Canada M5S 2Z5

THE TAPESTRY OF SAINT JOSEPH

"Chronological History of St. Joseph
and
His Apostle, Blessed Brother André"

Susan T. Stein

BT
690
S74
1991

NIHIL OBSTAT:
　James McGrath, J.C.D.
　Censor Librorum

November 2, 1990

IMPRIMATUR:
　Anthony J. Bevilacqua, D.D., J.C.D., J.D.
　Archbishop of Philadelphia

November 5, 1990

FIRST EDITION
© 1991 by Susan T. Stein
All rights reserved.

Library of Congress Catalog Card Number: 91-71601

ISBN: 0-9629293-0-1

Illustration by Frances Cassalia Castor

Produced by
Remco Worldservice Books, Inc., Book Packagers
Box 285, Abington, PA 19001

Printed in Hong Kong

Apostle Publishing
401 Parlin Place
Philadelphia, Pennsylvania 19116

1991

CONTENTS

Acknowledgments vii
Foreword ix
Introduction xi

    Preface 9
1. Background in the Infancy Narratives 10
2. Early Church 16
3. Middle Ages 30
4. Mid 15th and 16th Centuries 48
5. 17th Century 57
6. 18th Century 69
7. 19th Century through 1869 78
8. 19th Century from 1870 96
9. 20th Century through 1937 125
10. 20th Century: 1938 to 1958 146
11. 20th Century: Pope John XXIII to 1988 . 155
12. Summary 177
    Epilogue: Events of 1989 and 1990 182

Prayers and Devotions 213
Bibliography and Reference Sources 230
References 232
Index 235

DEDICATION

I dedicate this work to my beloved husband, John, who made it possible for me to bring St. Joseph and the Holy Family to the faithful. Thank you Jesus, Mary and Joseph, the ultimate example of family life. Thank you Brother André for interceding in John's life so that today, we can do the work you ask, spreading devotion to St. Joseph and the Holy Family.

ACKNOWLEDGMENTS

Special recognition is given to those dear friends who assisted in making this book possible. Without their love, support and prayers I might not have persevered. Attempting to name all who have been of great assistance, surely I would inadvertently overlook someone. Therefore, I will try to acknowledge those who gave support along the way.

Some friends must be given individual mention. Fr. William J. Cox, our spiritual director in Philadelphia, who through the love of God watches over John and me in our apostolate of spreading devotion to St. Joseph and Blessed Brother André. Our enthusiasm is kept in check by Father's suggestion "Do not try to write the script for God, as He needs no help."

A special note of appreciation to the Congregation of Holy Cross, our family away from home, at St. Joseph's Oratory in Montreal. Never have they failed to encourage and guide us in our apostolate. Fr. Marcel Lalonde, c.s.c., Rector of St. Joseph's Oratory, who some eight years ago sent us on our way by directing John and me "to tell everyone about St. Joseph and Blessed Brother André." Br. Robert Montcalm, c.s.c., in charge of the Cause of Brother André at the Oratory, who in spite of his hectic schedule, has taken on the task of being our "boss."

Br. Pierre-Paul Gougeon, c.s.c., director of the Associates of Brother André, has done much to assist in the research for this book. His gracious gift to begin a library on the Oratory in Philadelphia was most appreciated, without which, much information would not have been available.

Fr. Roland Gauthier, c.s.c., former Rector of the Oratory, founder and director of the Center for Research and Documentation on Saint Joseph as well as editor of "Cahiers de Joséphologie" (writings on St. Joseph). Without Father's kind direction, the book would not have been complete. It was quite an honor that he should take the time from his busy schedule to critique this work. He is internationally renowned in matters of theology and religious sciences, therefore, he has blessed us greatly with his love and cooperation.

Special gratitude is extended to Fr. Henri Bergeron, c.s.c. and Fr. René Gauvin, c.s.c. Fr. Bergeron authored many books relating to the Oratory, St. Joseph, Br. André and the Congregation of Holy Cross. These publications were of great importance in placing many events within their proper time frame. Fr. Gauvin was in charge of pilgrimages and it was with his guidance that John and I were named the official office in Philadelphia for the Oratory. With great love, I thank both these men who now guide us from Heaven.

All those we have come to know and love through their continued assistance, spreading the Good News and together growing closer to our Lord through devotion to Saint Joseph and Brother André.

To Joe and Dot Markmann, who know the power of Saint Joseph and Blessed Brother André and came forth to make the printing of the "Tapestry" a reality.

A thank you goes to Frances Cassalia Castor for the water color painting which makes the cover most impressive.

A loving thank you to my parents, William and Adeline Grier, for introducing me to this world, thus affording me the opportunity of membership in this apostolate.

FOREWORD

In our times, Saint Joseph is not a total unknown, but he is still misunderstood in many circles. In fact, a great number of people—even cultured people—refuse to recognize the privileged mission of this saint, because, they say, he is mentioned but a few times in the Gospels, and they in turn do not relate any of his words. Why then should this extremely silent one not be relegated to the shadows, and why should it not be sufficient to celebrate his feast only once a year?

It would be easy to retort that the Gospels do not dwell at length on the Virgin Mary either. One does not read in them numerous details of her life and of her special role in the history of salvation; a few sentences only, attributed to Mary, are quoted in the Gospels. Yet, the people of God have long since, and rightly so, developed a very particular and unremitting devotion to the Mother of God.

This answer, however, is insufficient. It is appropriate to recall that the Evangelists Matthew and Luke emphasize the personal dignity of St. Joseph, even if the words used to single out the characteristic features of the spiritual figure of this saint are few in number. According to the Scriptures, two titles are fittingly and exclusively his. He had the distinguished honour of having been chosen amongst all men to have been Mary's true husband and the virginal father of Jesus. In other words, he enjoyed a very peculiar privilege: to live for many years in the closest of relationships with Mary and Jesus, conversing informally and praying daily with them.

It should not be surprising therefore, if the Evangelist Matthew adds that Joseph was "an honest man", "a just man". Accordingly, it must be interpreted that Joseph was blessed with all of the virtues, for true justice consists in giving everyone his due, all while conscientiously fulfilling one's duty towards God and his fellow man. Therein lies the reason why Saint Joseph is considered the greatest of saints, second to the Virgin Mary only.

Because he is truly a part of the Holy Family of Nazareth, Joseph belongs to a special class. It was God Himself who assigned him that active and important role in the Mystery of the Incarnation by joining him closely and indissolubly to Mary and Jesus. Pope John Paul II, in his own way, reminded us of this mission by referring to this very truth twice in his Apostolic Exhortation, *Redemptoris Custos,* "on the person and mission of Saint Joseph in the life of Christ and of the Church" (August 15, 1989): God, he says, has entrusted to him "the custody of his most precious treasures".

Those who are interested in furthering their knowledge of this extraordinary saint, who was the head of the Holy Family, need only read attentively Mrs. Susan T. Stein's book. In it, they will find innumerable interesting details about the historical development of the devotion to Saint Joseph throughout the ages. Above all, however, the reader will realize that many renowned saints loved and venerated Saint Joseph and entrusted him with a choice place in their spiritual lives. In the book, the reader will also discover important information on the life and work of one of the 20th century's most dedicated apostles of Saint Joseph, namely Blessed Brother André of Montreal.

Pick up this book and read it deliberately; it will enable you to better understand and to better love Saint Joseph, the mighty protector of the Universal Church. You will also realize that Saint Theresa of

Avila was right when she wrote in her autobiography: "Because of my impressive experience of the goods this glorious Saint Joseph obtains from God, I had the desire to persuade everyone to be devoted to him. I have not known anyone truly devoted to him and rendering him special services who has not advanced more in virtue."

Roland Gauthier, C.S.C.

INTRODUCTION

All of us may be likened to single but distinct shades of thread which upon entering the Loom of Life, under the direction of the Master Weaver, God Almighty, become a part of His tapestry. At first glance we may see only a multiplicity of threads, some already in the loom and others about to enter. Then the weaver introduces a new single thread and this thread from the Master's spindle begins to bring all the threads into a semblance of order to produce one of the most beautiful and important scenes in the life of our Lord.

This single thread is called J O S E P H .

PREFACE

The threads of a tapestry are slow to form a picture. Thus is the life and cultus of St. Joseph. In this work the author will attempt to place the threads in their proper sequence through the centuries to produce the unusual scenes in the history of Saint Joseph.

We know the limited information given us in the infancy narratives of the Gospels. Beyond this information our Saint has remained fairly obscure until current times. However, it is recorded that many great saints had special regard and devotion to the father of Christ on earth. We shall deal with them as our text unfolds. The writings and thoughts of these individuals are well known to scholars and theologians. It is the author's intent to bring this knowledge to everyone.

Our desire is to present as completely as possible an accurate history of the church procedures regarding the position of Saint Joseph in our faith. The information contained herein is based on theological writings, opinions of many Popes and scholars, and is herewith presented with the express desire that the lay person as well as the theologian may gain more awareness of the beauty of Saint Joseph's cultus.

Many of the Ecclesiastical writers shared mutual feelings about St. Joseph with no personal knowledge of each other. In some cases their statements may lead the reader to weary of repetition. However, this repetition is strong evidence of their individual love of St. Joseph. The author has attempted to reduce as much as possible redundancy of these feelings.

CHAPTER ONE

To present the reader with a full appreciation of the life of Saint Joseph, we shall start with the Infancy Narratives from the Gospel.[1]

We begin with the genealogy of Joseph, thus the genealogy of Our Lord, Jesus Christ. According to Matthew's Gospel, Jacob is the father of Joseph[2], while in St. Luke's Gospel, we are told Joseph's father is Heli.[3] At first, this would appear to be a conflict as we can only have one father.

According to the Fathers and Doctors of the Church, there is no conflict, as Jacob was the natural father and Heli was the legal father (or father by affinity). To understand this terminology, we must refer to the Doctors of Holy Church. The first explanation of the mention of Heli, according to Julius Africanus, (as St. Luke mentioned) Heli took a wife and died, leaving no children. Now, the law provided that under such circumstances the widow could oblige the brother of her deceased husband to marry her, in order to raise up children to him. The widow of Heli, therefore, according to those who maintain this opinion, would have appealed to Jacob, whom they suppose to be Heli's brother, to take her in marriage, and thus Joseph, their child, was naturally the son of Jacob, but legally the son of Heli.[4]

The second explanation about Heli, as mentioned in St. Luke, is that he is none other than St. Joachim, the happy father of Mary, the august Queen of Heaven and earth. This opinion was alluded to by St. Augustine and others. All interpreters are agreed in recognizing the three names Heli, Eliachim and Joachim as synonymous, and as being used as such in scripture. Thus, it would be correct as Joseph was not his son by nature but his son by affinity, his son-in-law.

Therefore Luke would have traced Mary's genealogy without departing from the Hebrew custom, which was to never give genealogies on the woman's side.[5]

We will not attempt to make any further assumptions on this point. We know that Joseph was Jesus' foster-father on earth, following the lineage of David.

Our next reference to Saint Joseph is when the Virgin Mary, espoused to our Saint, is found to be with child by the power of the Holy Spirit. Joseph, her husband, an upright man unwilling to expose her to public ridicule, decided to divorce her quietly.[6] Saint Joseph, knowing it as not his child had no other solution.

Saint Joseph was confused by what he did not yet understand but was willing to fulfill the will of God. He did not wish to offend God by committing adultery, therefore he wished to cause the least harm possible to Mary, his wife.

Then, the angel of the Lord appeared in a dream and said "Joseph, son of David, have no fear about taking Mary as your wife. It is by the Holy Spirit that she has conceived this child. She is to have a son and you are to name him Jesus because he will save his people from their sins." All this was to fulfill what was said by the prophets: "The virgin shall be with child and give birth to a son, and they shall call him Emmanuel," a name that means "God is with us." So when Joseph awoke he did as the angel of the Lord had directed him and received her into his home as his wife. He had no relations with her at any time before the birth of her son, whom he named Jesus.[7]

They lived a virginal life, fulfilling the prophecies of old.

A decree was sent out by Caesar Augustus, ordering

a census. Everyone went to his own town to register. Joseph went to Bethlehem, the city of David, because he was of the house and lineage of David, to register with Mary, his espoused wife, who was with child. While they were there, she gave birth to her first-born son, wrapped him in swaddling clothes and laid him in a manger, since there was no room in the inn.[8]

The shepherds having received a message from the angel of the Lord, came to honor the baby and found Mary and Joseph, and the babe lying in a manger.[9]

It has been described that the shepherds came to adore Christ, representing the Jewish people.

On the eighth day, according to Hebrew law, was the time for the circumcision and the name Jesus was given to the child.[10]

When the time came to purify them according to the law of Moses, Mary and Joseph brought the baby to Jerusalem to be presented to the Lord, for it is written in the law of the Lord, "Every first-born male shall be consecrated to the Lord." They came to offer in sacrifice "a pair of turtledoves or two young pigeons," in accordance with the dictates in the law of the Lord.

There lived in Jerusalem at the time a certain man named Simeon. He was just and pious, and awaited the consolation of Israel, and the Holy Spirit was upon him. It was revealed to him by the Holy Spirit that he would not experience death until he had seen the Anointed of the Lord. He came to the temple inspired by the Spirit. And when the parents brought in the child, Jesus, to perform for him the customary ritual of the law, he took him in his arms and blessed God in these words:

"Now, Master, you can dismiss your servant in

peace; you have fulfilled your word. For my eyes have witnessed your saving deed displayed for all the peoples to see: A revealing light to the Gentiles, the glory of your people Israel."

Mary and Joseph were marveling at what was being said about the child. Simeon blessed them and said to Mary "This child is destined to be the downfall and the rise of many in Israel, a sign that will be opposed, and you yourself will be pierced with a sword — so that the thoughts of many hearts may be laid bare."

There was also a certain prophetess, Anna, daughter of Phanuel of the tribe of Asher, advanced in age, who remained in the temple, serving night and day, fasting and in prayer. Recognizing the child, she sang his praise and future glory.[11]

After the visit of the Magi, the angel of the Lord suddenly appeared in a dream to Joseph commanding: "Get up, take the child and his mother, and flee to Egypt. Stay there until I tell you otherwise. Herod is searching for the child to destroy him." Joseph got up and took the child and his mother and left that night for Egypt. He stayed there until the death of Herod, to fulfill what the Lord had said through the prophet: "Out of Egypt, I have called my son."[12]

The visit of the magi might be described as the recognition of the Messiah, the light of the world, to the Gentiles.

After Herod's death, the angel of the Lord appeared in a dream to Joseph, in Egypt with the command: "Get up, take the child and his mother, and set out for the land of Israel. Those who had designs on the life of the child are dead." He heard, however, that Archelaus had succeeded his father Herod as king of Judea, and he was afraid to go back there. Instead, because of a warning received in the dream, Joseph went to the region of Galilee. There he settled in a town called Nazareth. In this way what the prophets had said was fulfilled: "He shall be called a Nazarene."[13]

Again, Saint Joseph obeyed God's command without hesitation.

Mary and Joseph went to Jerusalem each year for the feast of the Passover. When Jesus was twelve, they came for the celebration as was the custom. When they were returning at the end of the feast, the child Jesus remained behind, unbeknownst to his parents. Thinking he was in the party, they continued a day, looking for him among the relatives and acquaintances.

Not finding Jesus, they returned to Jerusalem in search of Him. On the third day they found him in the temple sitting among the teachers, listening to them and asking them questions. All who heard him were amazed at his intelligence and his answers.

When his parents saw him they were astonished, and his mother said to him: "Son, why have you done this to us? You know that your father and I have been searching for you in sorrow." He said to them: "Why did you search for me? Did you not know I had to be in my Father's house?" But they did not understand the meaning of what he said to them.

He then went with them to Nazareth, and was obedient to them. His mother meanwhile kept all these things in her heart. Jesus, for his part progressed steadily in wisdom and age and grace before God and men.[14] This shows the two sides of Jesus, both God and man. It must have been difficult for Joseph and Mary to comprehend the apparent incongruity. Jesus was Mary's son by the Holy Spirit and Joseph's foster-son and yet, even knowing God's messages, they thought of Jesus as their own son. The reality is brought home when Jesus says "Did you not know that I had to be in my Father's house."

Finally, in reference to Saint Joseph's death, we assume that he died prior to Christ's ministry, because following the Temple finding scene there is no mention of St. Joseph in the New Testament. As was said of Jesus, "Where did this man get such wisdom and miraculous powers? Isn't this the carpenter's son? Isn't Mary known to be his mother?[15]

All who were present spoke favorably of him; they marveled at the appealing discourse which came from his lips. They also asked, "Is not this Joseph's son?"[16]

Philip sought out Nathanael and told him, "We have found the one Moses spoke of in the law — the prophets too — Jesus, son of Joseph, from Nazareth."[17]

When Jesus claimed, "I am the bread that came down from heaven." They kept saying: "Is this not Jesus, the son of Joseph? Do we not know his father and mother? How can he claim to have come down from heaven?"[18]

Joseph's death remains a secret, hidden from us, only known to God.

---

[1] All scripture references are from "The New American Bible", St. Joseph Edition
[2] Matthew 1:1–16 [3] Luke 3:23–38 [4] Life & Glories of St. Joseph, p.35–36
[5] Life & Glories of St. Joseph, p.38–39 [6] Matthew 1:18–19 and Luke 1:27
[7] Matthew 1:20–25 [8] Luke 2:1–7 [9] Luke 2:16 [10] Luke 2:21
[11] Luke 2:22–40 [12] Matthew 2:13–15 [13] Matthew 2:19–23 [14] Luke 2:41–52
[15] Matthew 13:55 [16] Luke 4:22 [17] John 1:45 [18] John 6:42

CHAPTER TWO

Saint Joseph has been so often referred to as the "most forgotten of the Holy Family." As St. Joseph's tapestry unfolds, the reader must bear in mind the attitudes of frustration and unrest existing at the time of the Espousal of Mary and Joseph. People had been praying and believing that the Messiah would appear in all glory and splendor and in basically one fell swoop, free them from the oppression of their Roman rulers. Never could they have imagined or accepted the plan of God to present for the salvation of all, a baby, the Son of God, to be born to a young couple living in their midst, coming into the world in such surroundings as a stable and from that humble birth change the course of history forever.

Those first, to adore our Lord after Joseph and Mary, were the shepherds. Those poor souls, pure of heart, not caught up in materialistic desires and able to understand, guided by the angel's message, what was happening. How proper it was that they should be the first to greet our Lord. Those whose minds were open, not filled with skepticism, but able to accept the simple truth that they were in the presence of the Savior. For others would have difficulty accepting the truth when confronted with it. But, is it any different today? This was better said almost one-thousand years before the birth of Jesus in Ecclesiastes 1:9, "What has been, that will be; what has been done, that will be done. Nothing is new under the Sun", including the skeptics.

When we look at the climate of history during First Century Christianity, we find the Apostles preaching the Doctrine of the Incarnation of the Son of God which took place in the pure womb of Mary, virgin before, during and after the birth of Jesus Christ, the

Savior of the world. It was believed by the Early Church, wise to downplay the role of St. Joseph in the Holy Family, better to assuage the fear of skeptics accepting the premise of a virginal relationship between Mary and Joseph, forgetting that this union was ordained by God. If St. Joseph had been given his true place from the beginning as the spouse of Mary and foster-father of Jesus, it might have compromised the doctrine of the Incarnation. The Early Church was also most cautious in honoring St. Joseph because they believed to do so might prejudice the dogma of Mary's virginity. A scripture passage from Acts 5:38,39 might be apropos at this time. "If their purpose or activity is human in its origins, it will destroy itself. If on the other hand, it comes from God, you will not be able to destroy them without fighting God himself."

We know St. Joseph was honored in the early centuries of the Church. This devotion was not practiced publicly at that time with the same solemnity as it is in our day, yet it was present in the hearts of those early Christians. St. Joseph was chosen by God, therefore God kept him in the minds of the faithful. The heretics would be defeated. A time will come when he will no longer be forgotten. Time may take centuries, but as was said in II Peter 3:8, "In the Lord's eyes, one day is as a thousand years and a thousand years are as a day." Therefore what may seem slow to us is in accord with God's Plan.

The Early Church was predominantly occupied with the study and interpretation of Holy Scripture, specifically the Gospels. Although mention of St. Joseph is limited in the Gospels, what the scholars have written is with the greatest reverence, honoring, praising and extolling his virtues.

Among the earliest scholars were St. Justin (c.100–165) and Origen, or Origenes (c.185–c.254).

Following in the fourth and fifth centuries were St. Epiphanius, St. John Chrysostom and St. John Damascene in the Eastern Church, St. Ambrose, St. Jerome, St. Augustine and St. Hilary in the Western Church. All rendered excellent testimony of their veneration for St. Joseph in their writings.

Joseph was venerated in pictures and bas reliefs in the catacombs. Private oratories contain abundant memorials to him. His name was engraved in the hearts of the faithful and sculptured in marble and bronze in the underground cradle of the Roman Church. The Greek Epigraph inscribed on a gem of the 4th or 5th century, which was brought to light by Cavedoni, proved the loving confidence in St. Joseph held by the early Christians. On it was written: "O Joseph, assist me in my labors and give me grace."

In a fresco at Rome, in the cemetery of St. Priscilla, which belongs to the first century or beginning of the second, St. Joseph is represented standing near the Virgin Mother with the Infant in her arms. In the cemetery of St. Callistus is to be seen another second century fresco showing St. Joseph between the Virgin and the Child. St. Joseph is pictured on various tombs of the first four centuries as well as in the mosaics of St. Mary Major (c.360).

The author would like to offer some thought to dispel the idea that St. Joseph was an old man. Whenever a really aged person is mentioned in the Gospels, the Evangelists do refer to their old age as in the case of Zachary, Elizabeth and the Prophetess Anna. St. Luke simply says that the Blessed Virgin was espoused to a man (1:27) not to *an old man* like Zachary (1:18), or to one *advanced in years* like Elizabeth. The early Christians were nearer in time to St. Joseph than the apocryphists, and we believe better informed. The Talmud recommends 18 up to the age of 20 for marriage and thus the early paintings in the catacombs show St. Joseph young and beardless, not elderly.

As we proceed, we will present the ecclesiastical writers and the honor they gave St. Joseph within their chronological time frame. The reader is asked to understand that the majority of what was said and written was to dispel the apocryphal gospels of the third through sixth centuries (of which there were five gospels). The apocryphists expounded on St. Joseph as a doddering old man and a widow with many children. They proposed that he was chosen by the high priests of the Temple to safeguard Mary's virginity in her predicament. Fortunately for us, these have been proven as falsehoods devised to explain what seemed beyond explanation at the time.

The reader will find there are certain areas of discussion, specifically, Joseph's love for Mary, his virginity and his faith which are expounded upon again and again by each subsequent scholar. They apparently did this to help the faithful realize the falsehoods prevalent during the Early Church. We shall not dwell on these falsehoods in detail. They did their damage once, let us not add confusion to our dear St. Joseph.

The Early Church preserves little documentation, however we will present as concise as possible the data available. Please understand, we honor Jesus by honoring his mother and father; also we honor Mary by honoring St. Joseph.

St. Justin, Martyr

St. Justin, Martyr (c.100–165) was converted to Christianity c.130 and defended it in Asia Minor and Rome where he suffered his martyrdom. While speaking on St. Joseph's occupation, St. Justin says, "When John first met Jesus, he knew him as the son of Joseph, the carpenter. Jesus Himself was thought to be a carpenter, for while He lived among men He had performed carpenter's work, making ploughs and yokes, teaching us to lead just lives free from idleness." Ancient pictures representing St. Joseph with carpenter's tools confirm the testimony of St. Justin.

St. Justin further indicates that both in beauty and in bodily appearance he was most like our Lord; and this was fitting indeed that no suspicion might arise respecting his paternity or the virtue of the Mother of the Divine Child. Although little has been preserved regarding his writings, what we have is important as he lived at a time and was able to converse with those who knew the Apostles.

St. Anastasia

St. Anastasia (Martyred c.302) heroically gave her life during the brutal persecutions of the Roman Emperor, Diocletian. This emperor reigned from 284–305 in Sirmium, an important city in ancient Pannonia, as well as in the city of Split in Dalmatia, now part of Yugoslavia. After the burning of his palace in Split, for which the Christians were blamed, the last and most terrible of the Roman persecutions against the Church commenced in 302.

A noble Roman matron named Apollonia built St. Anastasia Church in Rome and interred St. Anastasia's body there. We include this information in our journey through history as this church contains a precious relic, St. Joseph's pallium or mantle, venerated because it must have enveloped the Divine Infant when clasped in Joseph's arms. An inscription in Latin on a stone attests to the antiquity of the relics as there is also the Blessed Virgin's veil and a portion of wood from the Cross; thus the Holy Family always remains together.

Early honor was paid to St. Joseph in Syria and

Persia. In the Syrian calendar, the seventh Sunday before Christmas was the feast of the "Revelation to Joseph, Spouse of the Blessed Virgin". The Greek Church celebrated the cultus of St. Joseph early in the 4th century.

In Bethlehem, guides still point to a location on the slope of a hill between the Grotto of Milk and the Great Church of our Lord's Nativity which was built by St. Helen, mother of Constantine, as the site of St. Joseph's house. It was once an Oratory but now is no longer in existance. Also at Nazareth, about 200 feet from the Basilica of the Annunciation there is still located St. Joseph's workshop, which is now also a Catholic Church.

St. Athanasius

St. Athanasius (c.296–May 2, 373) was Bishop of Alexandria c.330. During his lifetime he earned the title of "Father of Orthodoxy". St. Joseph was honored among the Copts (the native Egyptians of the Christian faith). Because of St. Joseph's travels to Egypt, he is recognized as having brought the knowledge of Jesus and Mary into that country long before St. Athanasius sent missionaries to instruct the inhabitants of Alexandria in the Christian faith.

St. Ephrem

St. Ephrem (306–373) said: "How can anyone ever properly praise St. Joseph, whom You, O true only-begotten Son of the Eternal Father, has chosen as Your foster-father."

St. Ambrose

St. Ambrose (c.340–397) was the Bishop of Milan from 374 to 397. He observed that St. Joseph, next to Mary, was the most eminent among the saints and was born for the profit of all, since he was destined by God to be the patron of all Christians.[1] As St. Ambrose said: "How, then, could it be possible that his nativity should pass unnoticed and not be the cause of joy in Heaven?"

St. Ambrose spoke of Adam and Eve as "Two in one flesh". Of Joseph and Mary, he said they were "Two in one spirit". From the moment of their alliance the souls of St. Joseph and Mary possessed one same heavenly and divine life.

Lastly, St. Ambrose said "since it is written that 'God will do the will of them that fear Him', how can He refuse to do the will of St. Joseph who nourished Him for so long, working by the sweat of his brow?"

St. John Chrysostom

St. John Chrysostom (c.349–407) invites us to witness the purity of St. Joseph's soul, never stained by the corruption of sin.[2]

The Greeks called St. Joseph the partner and mediator of the mystery of the Incarnation. Further, St. Joseph was espoused to the Mother of God so that he might be Her tutor and guardian, and an aid near to Her in every vicissitude of life. He further points out emphatically that, save bodily generation, everything that makes a father, pertains to St. Joseph, fosterer, guardian and teacher of the Son of God.

The Angel's Message: [3]

The Angel sought out Joseph when he was very troubled in mind. . . . Notice this Holy man's forbearance. . . . He does nothing to chastise his wife, he does not even tell her the grave suspicions that have been aroused in his mind. He keeps all these things to himself, hiding his anxiety and suffering, even from Mary. . . . Joseph did not confide his fears to anybody. He kept them locked up in his heart, and yet he heard an angel speaking to him about them. Surely this is unquestionable proof that the angel was sent by God, for God alone can read the depths of the heart. . . . So wise was Joseph's behavior that it shows how good and virtuous a man he was. . . .

"Keep the wife whom you are thinking of putting away," the angel said to him, "for She is given to you, not by Her parents, but by God himself. He does not give Her, that there may be bodily union between you, but that you may dwell together in fellowship; and He joins you with Her through the ministry of my words." Just as Christ Himself later entrusted Her to the care of His disciple, John, so now the angel gives Her to Her husband that She may have joy in his company. . . .

That Joseph might be fully reassured, the angel spoke of the future as well as of the past: "She shall bring forth a Son, and thou shalt call his name Jesus. You must not think that, because this Child is conceived of the Holy Spirit, He is nothing to do with you: you have to look after Him and care for Him in every way. Although you have no part in his begetting and Mary is forever maiden, nevertheless you stand in a father's place toward this Child in all that does not touch the Virgin's dignity, and it is for you to name Him. You shall be the first to call Him by His name; and though He is not your son you will always show Him a father's love and care. Therefore, you will name Him yourself, that He and you may be more closely united."

The Holy Spirit, speaking through the Prophets, spoke of the Redeemer under many names. "His name shall be called Emmanuel," we read in Isaiah, and elsewhere, "His name will be called Wonderful, God the Mighty, the Father of the world to come, the Prince of Peace." In giving the name of Jesus to the Redeemer of mankind, Saint Joseph uncovered to the world all these mysteries unknown to the world or at least undiscovered by it. It was a tremendous honor to be the instrument of the Holy Spirit in this event. No one less than Saint Joseph could reveal this adorable name to the world and give it to the Infant God.

St. Chrysostom speaks of St. Joseph as a 'Just' man and that the Holiness of St. Joseph surpasses the holiness of all other creatures except Mary. His holiness made him free from all evil thoughts, words and actions enabling him to be in union with God. His intimacy with the Son of God, made him a man of unwavering faith with deep humility. His unquestionable obedience and love of God, with a high sense of Justice made him to be called a 'Just Man' by the Apostle.

The Role of Mary and Joseph with the Child as a family unit was predestined by God. St. John Chrysostom points to four reasons for this to be so. First, the royal descent of the Virgin Mary would be patently clear, both St. Matthew and St. Luke make a special point that St. Joseph was "of the house and family of David". Thus it is clear that Mary too was of royal stock, since it was the inveterate custom of the Jews that marriage should take place between members of the same tribe. Second, Mary's honor would not have to suffer when she bore her child, nor would she incur punishment from the law. Evidently to have conceived and given birth to a child without being married would have been the equivalent of having incurred public disgrace. For although her virginity was to be preserved, and She, filled with grace, was to be the Mother of God, people would only see what was before their eyes. And it would be difficult for a woman to avoid dishonor and defamation in a small town by having a child without a father. Jesus' position would not then be within the rules of the juridical order of His people and of His time. From the beginning He would have been, in a sense, discredited.

The third reason is that an older man, however good and well disposed he might be, would be unlikely to have the energy and enterprise needed for the difficult and hurried flight into Egypt, there to begin a new life, with no assets but his own work, in the midst of foreign people and in a land that favored pagan customs. It would be rough. It would hardly bespeak a tranquil life. Chrysostom adds the fourth reason from St. Ignatius of Antioch: "it would be to conceal from the devil the birth of the Messiah." For when the angel Gabriel announced the mystery of the Incarnation to Mary, she was already engaged to Joseph. The betrothal was really the marriage, the "wedding" being only its perfection.

St. Augustine

St. Augustine (c.354–430) said that St. Joseph merited the title of father of Jesus more than do other fathers in the natural order. His line of reasoning is interesting. It is well recognized that a man to whom God gives a son, born of a Christian marriage is esteemed to be more worthy of the title father than those whose children have been the fruit of a union unsanctified by wedlock. Chastity contributes to the honor of paternity and confirms the justice of its claims. If anyone should have a son of his legitimate spouse, preserving at the same time inviolable virginity, as Joseph did in his union with the Mother of God, there would be a higher reason for calling such a one father than any who have ever lived in the bonds of matrimony.

With the possibility of future developments, Augustine speaks of the relations between Mary and the Church, each maiden and each mother, containing the seed of the idea that Joseph, guardian of Mary and Jesus, must be the guardian of the Church[4] and Her children, the brethren of Jesus. St. Augustine believed this but dared not dream; for at that time all his contemporaries still thought of Joseph as a lesser figure, lost in the radiance of Jesus and His Mother.

St. Augustine says that our aim should be to do God's will in all things, accepting from His hand whatever He wills to send us. In dealing with trials and tribulations, we will find that not all of us are masters of ourselves to such an extent as to rejoice in our tribulations. If we could, we would become more like Joseph and Mary. Therefore, at least we can try to accept our tribulations and bear them with patience and resignation. God wants us to do so and gives us the grace to do so. Resignation to God's Holy Will does not mean that we should not feel repugnance to suffering, or that we should not seek relief in our suffering. What St. Augustine says concerning the tears which we shed over the dead applies here. He says, "that it is better for the human heart to find consolation in tears, than to cease to be a human heart by not shedding tears."

On the resurrection of St. Joseph, St. Augustine felt that when Christ raised Mary from the dead and took Her up into heaven, He did so to honor Her because She was His Mother, in fulfillment of God's own command: "Honor thy father and thy mother" (Exod. 20:12). This motive would also apply to St. Joseph, for though he was not the father of Jesus according to the flesh, he discharged all the duties and offices of a loving father toward his foster son. Since Jesus wished to honor His Blessed Mother by raising Her from the dead and taking Her up to Heaven, body and soul, we cannot imagine that Jesus would not wish to bestow a similar honor on St. Joseph who was His foster-father and after Mary the greatest of all saints.... According to this authority, St. Joseph was the father of Jesus in the most perfect manner possible. And this he was in three ways: by love, by care and by authority.

Devotion to the saints consists chiefly of three, things: admiration of their greatness, imitation of their virtues and invocation of their help. But of these three, the most important is imitation of their virtues. St. Augustine tells us that "true devotion consists of imitating the one we honor."

The Fathers of the Church assume that St. Joseph held the obvious explanation of Mary's condition and that he bore the terrible trial without being dragged down by any natural reaction. Based on that premise, St. Augustine wrote: "He knew, indeed, that she was not bearing his child and therefore took her for an adulterous.... As a husband he was very upset. But as a just man he shows himself not to be cruel. This man's holiness was so great that he neither wished to keep an adulterous with him, nor did he presume to punish her by making public her dishonor...."

St. Jerome

St. Jerome (340–420) was of the opinion that St. Joseph's sepulchre was included within the limits of the Garden of Gethsemane. And it was no mystery that Jesus made the choice of that spot for prayer, especially on the night of his agony. Possibly, He desires us to seek St. Joseph when we are in our last agony, and to enjoy the consolation of his patronage at that dread hour.[5]

Tradition says that Joseph went to Jerusalem with Mary and Jesus to celebrate the feast of the unleavened bread, the Pasch, which was always kept at the full moon following the 14th, thus died on the 19th of March as the Church holds. The Roman Martyrology says "In Judea, the birthday of St. Joseph, spouse of Blessed Mary the Virgin, Confessor." Had St. Joseph died in Nazareth, the notation would have been Galilee not Judea. Tradition holds that the tomb was in the Valley of Josaphat, which was thought to be in the Cedron (Kidron) Valley on the eastern side of Jerusalem. According to John 18:1 "Jesus went out with his disciples across the Kidron Valley. There was a garden there and He and His disciples entered it." (This was the evening of the Agony.)

When St. Jerome was called to Rome during the Pontificate of St. Damasus, he celebrated mass during the three years at the altar of St. Anastasia Church, where St. Joseph's precious relic is preserved.

In defining "St. Joseph was a just man", St. Jerome says St. Joseph was the possessor of all virtues — not of one virtue or of many virtues or of a great many virtues or of a very great many virtues, but of all virtues without exception. And not only this, but that he practised all virtues in a most perfect manner. What more could be said of any man than to say that he possessed all virtues and practiced them in the most perfect manner possible! Greater praise than this could not be given to anyone. Hence there can be no doubt that St. Joseph corresponded with the grace which he received from God, and this grace is the greatest bestowed on any man after that given to our Blessed Lady.

St. Jerome opposed the theory that St. Joseph was an old man and had children already. Fortunately, that theory did not survive. He also emphasized the fact that "God confided His Virgin Mother to a virgin." St. Jerome further states: "Since St. Joseph was a just man, holy and perfect in all virtues, it is certain that nothing that savored of impurity ever entered his life, and since there is nothing on record that he ever had any other spouse than the Virgin Mary, it is also certain that he remained a virgin all his life." He maintained that not only Mary, but Her spouse was always a virgin, so that of this virginal marriage, a virginal Son might be born.

St. Jerome gives the first reason for the marriage of Mary and Joseph through the genealogy of Joseph thus Mary's origin might be known. For with the Jews, genealogy was always reckoned through the father instead of the mother, since father and mother had to be of the same tribe and family. A second reason for Mary's marriage was that she might not be looked upon as a public sinner and stoned to death according to the law. The third reason given was that Mary might have a husband to help Her, to protect Her, to defend Her, to console Her, to support Her in Her needs, in Her difficulties, such as in Her journey to Egypt and Her sojourn there.

St. Peter Chrysologus

St. Peter Chrysologus (406–450) was of the opinion that St. Joseph was destined to occupy on earth the place of the Eternal Father, and to represent Him in relation to His Divine Son. Now, perpetual virginity shines among the attributes of the Divine Paternity; wherefore Joseph, the representative on earth of the Divine Paternity, must, next to Mary, possess the beautiful virtue of virginity in the highest degree.

All footnotes are based on references by number and page number.

[1, 4] Not to be officially declared until 1870

[2] (#26, p. 391) Author is unable to fully verify this reference.

[3] (#20, p. 55) Excerpts from the Homily IV on Matthew

[5] (#26, p. 410) Author is unable to fully verify this reference

CHAPTER THREE

As we enter the beginning of the Middle Ages which the scholars refer to as the Dark Ages (476–1000), that portion of the Middle Ages characterized by the age of intellectual stagnation, widespread ignorance and poverty and cultural decline, we find the information available is limited. The Early Church maintained devotion to St. Joseph, although it remained fairly hidden until the 8th century. The Greek Church was the first to practice devotion openly in the 9th century, and Egypt seems to have been the home of the earliest cultus of St. Joseph.

Venerable Bede

Venerable Bede (c.672–735) considered that it was probably by Divine disposition that St. Joseph's death occurred at the season of the Pasch, in order that, according to his desire, he might be buried with his ancestors.

When Bede spoke on the scripture "Blessed is the womb that bore Thee and the breasts that nourished Thee. But Jesus said, rather Blessed are they who hear the word of God and keep it" (Luke 11:27,28), He gives the following explanation. He says that Jesus agrees, that Mary was Blessed because She bore Him in Her womb, but that She was still more Blessed because She bore Him in Her heart by means of love. Now, if Jesus considered Mary more His mother by reason of the great love which She had for Him, must we not conclude that, for the same reason, Joseph was more the father of Jesus, since after Mary, he loved Jesus more than any other saint loved Him?

St. Joseph, the Hymnographer

St. Joseph the Hymnographer (816–886) had great devotion to St. Joseph. He was one of the early theologians to take the name of Joseph in honor of our Saint. Through his influence the Greek Church celebrated the feast of St. Joseph on the Sunday after the Nativity and he gives a canon for that Sunday which concludes: "Thou O Godbearing Joseph, was the guardian of the Virgin who preserved virginity intact. Be thou, with Her mindful of us, O Joseph." There is record of some of his hymns being entered into the Byzantine liturgy.

Great Schism of 1054

During this period came the Great Schism of 1054. This conflict between the Churches of the East and the West created a difference generated from what was central to their religious life. At this time the East opposed the increase in power and claims of the Roman bishop. The theological differences were mainly in the way they were perceived. Theology in the East was more mystical and aesthetic, whereas in the West it was more dogmatic and rational. The center of religious life in the East is the icon; of the West, doctrine. This is one of the major events taking place in history at the end of the Dark Ages which created discention within the Church.

Church history has held little regarding St. Joseph, however, March 19th, the solemn feast of St. Joseph was listed in several churches as far back as the 10th century. We come to the end of the Dark Ages, which is followed by that period known as Medieval History. In art we find three basic divisions: Early Christian, Romanesque (11th and 12th centuries) and Gothic (between the 12th and 16th centuries). This indicates the wide diversification during this period of over 1000 years. Those scholars speaking of St. Joseph become more prolific, his devotion begins to grow ever so slowly.

St. Peter Damian

St. Peter Damian (1007–1072) asserted in a letter to Nicholas (Pope 1059–61) and in his work on the celibacy of the clergy, that the Son of God, not content with having a Virgin for His mother, willed that he, who represented His father, should also be a virgin. This great Doctor of the Church does not hesitate to qualify this belief as the "Faith of the Church."

St. Bernard

St. Bernard (1090–1153) says that while the first Joseph (of the Old Testament) receives from God the intelligence for the interpretation of dreams, to the second, He gives both the knowledge and the participation of heavenly mysteries. The former passed from the obscurity of a prison to the splendors of a court. Our St. Joseph passed from the sorrows of exile to the celestial mansions, with the true regal dignity of reputed father of the King of Kings, spouse of the Queen of Heaven, and most powerful Patron of the Universal Church.[6]

St. Bernard is the author of the "memorare" to our Blessed Mother and also the author of the antiphon "O fortunate man, Blessed Joseph, to whom it was given to see the God whom many kings yearned to see and did not see, to hear the God whom many kings yearned to hear and did not hear; Joseph was fortunate not only to see and hear, but to carry, to kiss, to clothe and to protect Him".

He considered that St. Joseph was united with the Savior in the quality of a coadjutor, whom God gave to His Son as His associate in the most magnificent of all His works, the Redemption of men. . . .

In Joseph, the Lord found a man after His own heart to whom He could safely entrust the most holy and hidden secrets. To him, God showed the hidden things of His wisdom and gave him knowledge of a mystery that was hidden from the great ones of the earth. Joseph was the witness to the fulfillment of the promise.

St. Bernard says, if you want to form an idea of St. Joseph's greatness, consider that by a Divine privilege he merited the title "Father of Jesus." The great patriarch Joseph was sold by his brothers in Egypt; our Saint has inherited not only his name, but even more, his power, his innocence, and his sanctity. As the patriarch Joseph stored the wheat not for himself, but for the people in their time of need, so St. Joseph had received a heavenly commission to watch over the Living Bread not for himself alone, but for the entire world. . . .

Church history tells us the oldest church bearing St. Joseph's name in Italy, was a parish church in Bologna about 1129. It claims the distinction to have included the name of St. Joseph in the Litany of the Saints in the year 1350. A titular feast of St. Joseph was celebrated in this church as indicated from its constitution drawn up by the Servite Fathers who were its custodians at that time.

St. Albert the Great

St. Albert the Great (c.1206–80) said St. Joseph could be called the support of the whole human race because, in taking charge of the upbringing of Jesus Christ, he contributed much to the salvation of men. . . .

St. Albert calls St. Joseph the advocate and patron of the Blessed Virgin because he sheltered Her from the penalties which Her Divine Delivery would have brought upon Her.... St. Albert continues, this marriage was ordained in order to make men regard St. Joseph as their father, even as they recognize Mary as their Mother.

He believed, any priest without devotion to St. Joseph would be an anomaly.... He also assures all priests, that St. Joseph must be regarded as the exemplar of those who hold any position in the church. You cannot excuse yourselves from choosing St. Joseph as the object of your particular devotion. You, who so often touch the body of Jesus Christ, should love this saint, who was the first of all men who had the honor to receive the Savior into his hands.

St. Bonaventure

St. Bonaventure (1217–1274) became a Bachelor of Scripture and lectured on the Gospel of St. Luke. According to him the union of Mary and Joseph was the purest form of Marriage guided by the Holy Spirit. Bonaventure speaks very highly in praise of St. Joseph, particularly about the interior life of our saint.

St. Bonaventure contributed much to the writings of the Franciscan Fathers during the Medieval period.

St. Thomas Aquinas

St. Thomas Aquinas (c.1225–74) said that "some saints are privileged to extend to us their patronage with particular efficacy in certain needs, but not in others; but our holy patron, St. Joseph, has the power to assist us in all cases, in every necessity, in every undertaking."...

He says: Since Jesus from the cross confided His virgin Mother to a virgin, St. John, is it possible that the Eternal Father should treat Mary with less reverence by giving Her a man who was not a virgin for a husband? . . . No, as Mary was the first among women, Joseph was the first among men to give prominence to the vow of perpetual virginity by making and keeping it.

St. Thomas teaches that, according to His nature and office, Christ is the only primary mediator of God and men, but that there are secondary mediators and intercessors, such as men on earth and saints and angels in Heaven. Of all our secondary mediators and intercessors, our Blessed Lady, the Mother of God, is the first and the greatest. . . . Our next greatest secondary mediator and intercessor is St. Joseph, the spouse of Mary and the foster-father of Jesus. . . .

Those whom God elects and designs for some great work, He also prepares and disposes to fit them for its performance. St. Thomas adds, that God gives grace to each proportionally to the office which he is chosen.

House of Loreto

A question asked quite frequently by those of the Christian faith is "whatever happened to the little home in Nazareth where Jesus grew up under the loving care of Joseph and the Holy Mother". This brings us to discuss the Holy House of Loreto, perhaps the most revered relic and most famous place of pilgrimage after the Holy Sepulchre and St. Peter's in Rome.

This Holy House in Nazareth was revered from the time of the Apostles. The house was a stone edifice 31 feet by 13 feet. St. Helena (c.300) built a church around it, which was named St. Mary's. It is recorded that St. Luke made a statue of Mary carved of cedar.

Multitudes of pilgrims came to visit this Holy House. However, power plays for control of the shrines of Christianity, in spite of the efforts of the Crusaders, left the control in Saracen hands, who profaned the Holy Places.

God was not willing to have the Holy House exposed to the profanation of the Infidels. After the fall of the Latin Kingdom of Jerusalem in 1291, it is related that angels transported the house to an area in Dalmatia (Rieka, Yugoslavia) on May 10, 1291. The miracles which occurred daily in the house, the judicial investigation which deputies from Galilee made in Nazareth in order to establish the validity of the removal of this Holy House to Dalmatia, as well as the universal belief of the people from all nations who came to venerate it, seemed to be incontestable proofs of the validity of this extraordinary happening.

Nevertheless, it pleased God to give another proof that all Italy and Dalmatia would witness. After three years and seven months, the Holy House was transported across the Adriatic Sea to the territory of Recanati in the midst of a forest belonging to a pious and noble widow named Lauretta. This work occured on Dec. 10, 1294 when members of the family of Anggeloi were prominent in the Byzantine Empire.

The Dalmatians were so grieved over their loss of the Holy House that in order to console themselves, they built a church which they consecrated to the Mother of God on the sight where the Holy House had been. It is in the charge of the Franciscans. On its door was placed this inscription (English translation) "The sacred house of Nazareth once was here, and is now in the locality of Recanati." Many Dalmatians went to Italy to make their home near the new location of the Holy House.

The news of this unusual event soon spread throughout Christendom, and a multitude of pilgrims came from many countries of Europe to honor the Holy House of Loreto, as it was called. To establish more fully the truth of the miracle, the inhabitants of the province sent sixteen of their most qualified people to Dalmatia, and afterwards to Nazareth, to make a new investigation. The delegation verified the measurements of the Holy House against the foundations in Nazareth, where they found an inscription stating that the church had disappeared.

God Himself intervened to make it manifest beyond all doubt, by suddenly removing, twice in succession, the Holy House in the territory of Recanati. When the forest of Loreto had become infested with thieves, who threatened pilgrims, the Holy House was again miraculously transported to a hill on August 10, 1295 which belonged to two brothers of the Antici family. When the brothers fought each other over division of the offerings of the pilgrims, the Holy House was transported to a place on the main road. It was transported to its present site on Dec. 2, 1295. The people of Recanati, recognizing a miracle, surrounded the Holy House with a wall and provided for its maintenance.

The stone and mortar with which the House was built are not known locally but are common around Nazareth; and the fact that the House has never had foundations where it now stands agrees with the tradition that it was moved bodily from another site. The house is of domestic not ecclesiastical origin and appears to have once been divided into three rooms.

Pope Benedict, the Bollandists, as well as many Pontifical Bulls, established as a fact worthy of faith, that the Sanctuary of Our Lady of Loreto, venerated by Catholics everywhere, is the sacred house in which the Word of God was conceived, and which sheltered Jesus, Mary and Joseph during the Hidden Life of the Savior of mankind.

St. Margaret of Cortona

St. Margaret of Cortona (1247–1297) relates that our Lord spoke to her saying "I wish, O Margaret, to make known to you how greatly the devotion you have to My foster-father pleases Me; but I desire that every day you would render him whatever tribute of praise and honor you can, as he is most dear to My heart."

St. Bridget of Sweden

St. Bridget of Sweden (1303–1373) relates that many times the most holy Virgin incited the panegyric of Her spouse, in order to increase devotion to him. It was related by St. Bridget that the Mother of God called St. Joseph Her dear spouse, and made such a magnificent eulogy of him that St. Bridget's admiration and love for the father of Jesus was greatly increased for the rest of her life.

St. Bridget tells us in her Revelations, that the Blessed Mother still calls St. Joseph Her beloved spouse. It is incomprehensible that the two should be parted. Now, since the Blessed Virgin is the general depository of all riches of Heaven, we must conclude that St. Joseph shares in the glory of distributing them among us. As the Blessed Virgin Mary said to St. Bridget, "St. Joseph was so reserved and careful in his speech that not one word ever issued from his mouth that was not good and holy, nor did he ever indulge in unnecessary or less charitable conversation. He was most patient and diligent in bearing fatigue. He practiced extreme poverty. He was most meek in bearing injuries. He was strong and constant against My enemies. He was the faithful witness of the wonders of Heaven, being dead to the flesh and the world, living only for God and for Heavenly goods, which were the only things he desired. He was perfectly conformed to the divine will and so resigned to the dispositions of Heaven, that he often repeated: 'May the will of God be ever done in me!' He rarely spoke with men, but continually with God, Whose will he desired to perform. Wherefore, He now enjoys great glory in Heaven."

Great Schism of the West

The Great Schism of the West began with the death of Pope Gregory XI in 1378. At this time there were rival popes at Avignon, France and in Rome, with there respective adherents. Each rival succession was maintained until the convocation of the Council of Pisa in 1409, at which time both reigning Popes were deposed. A third pope was elected as sole Pope. Pope Benedict XIII of Avignon refused to comply, so the schism continued until 1417 with the election of Martin V by the Council of Constance.

In 1399 the Franciscans celebrated the feast of St. Joseph as laid down by their general chapter and used the "common of a confessor" in their liturgical text of the mass.

St. Bernardine of Siena

St. Bernardine of Siena (1389–1444), that great glory of the Seraphic Order and great lover of St. Joseph, delivered an admirable sermon in honor of St. Joseph after declaring his conviction that Joseph enjoyed the same privilege as Mary in the resurrection of his body. He concludes saying, as this Holy Family . . . that is Christ, the Virgin and Joseph . . . had been united in a laborious life and in loving grace while on Earth. So also their bodies and souls reign together in Heaven in loving glory, according to that Apostolic Rule: "as you are partakers of the sufferings, so shall you be also of the consolation." While he was preaching in Padua, he declared that the body and soul of St. Joseph were both glorified in Heaven. A rich cross of gold was seen over the head of the preacher, proving to the very eyes of those who surrounded him, the truth which he was conveying to their ears.

St. Bernardine said that if you compare St. Joseph to the whole Church of Christ is he not the special and chosen being of whom and under whom the Lord was introduced into the world with becoming dignity? If all the faithful are debtors to the Virgin Mother for being made worthy through Her to receive the Redeemer. There can be no doubt that next to the Mother of God we owe to St. Joseph our special homage and veneration.

The following is a sermon on St. Joseph given by St. Bernardine: Whenever special blessings are conferred on any rational creature, whenever anyone is divinely chosen for some particular grace or for some exalted position, that person likewise receives all the gifts needed for that high position, and receives them in abundance... This was true in a marked degree of St. Joseph, the supposed father of our Lord Jesus Christ and the true husband of the Queen of the World and Mistress of the Angels; he was chosen by the Eternal Father to be the faithful teacher and guardian of His greatest treasures, namely, of His own Son and of Joseph's Bride. And this trust he carried out with complete faithfulness, so that the Lord says, "Good and faithful servant, enter thou into the joy of your Lord..."

The marriage between Mary and Joseph was a real marriage, entered into under Divine Inspiration; and marriage involves so close a union of souls that bridegroom and bride are said to be one person, which may be called the perfection of unity.... can, then, any discerning person imagine that the Holy Spirit would join in that union the soul of a maiden to a soul that was not closely like Her in the things of virtue? Therefore do I believe that this man, the holy Joseph, was graced with perfect virginity, with the deepest humbleness, with the most burning love and charity toward God, with the loftiest contemplation. . . . the Virgin knew that he was given Her by the Holy Spirit to be Her husband and the faithful protector of Her virginity. She knew that he was given, moreover, to share in devoted love and tender care for God's Divine Son. Therefore, do I believe that She loved St. Joseph fondly and with heartfelt affection. . .

Joseph had a burning love for Christ. Who, I ask, would deny that Christ, whether as a child or man, would arouse the most unutterable feelings of joy and happiness in one who lived in intimacy with Him and held Him in his arms, who experienced Jesus' loving looks and embraces, who listened to His speech? How sweet must have been the kisses Joseph received from Him! How moving to hear the Child murmur the name of father, how delightful to feel His gently encircling arms! Or again, when the Child was growing bigger, but was wearied with much walking on the journeys that they took, think how Joseph was filled with compassion and rested Him in his arms. For Joseph had for Jesus all the fullness of adoptive love, as for a darling Son given him by the Holy Spirit in his maiden Bride.

The wise Mother knew the depth of Joseph's affection, and so She says to Her Son, Jesus, when She found Him in the Temple, "Son, why have you done this to us? Behold, Your father and I have been seeking You sorrowing." To understand this correctly, we must remember that Christ has two forces within Him, namely, sweetness and sorrow. . . . and since the most holy Joseph experienced these two forces in a wonderful way, the Blessed Virgin calls him Christ's father in a special sense.

This is the only place where we read that She called

St. Joseph the father of Jesus. And She did so because his sorrow at the loss of the Child showed the fatherly love he had for Him. According to human law (which God approves) a man can adopt the child of another family as his own. How much more truly then ought the Son of God be called the Son of Joseph, given to him in his most holy Bride in the wondrous mystery of their virginal marriage; and it must indeed be believed that in Joseph there was a father's love and sorrow toward the beloved Jesus. . . .

There can be no doubt that in Heaven, Christ treats Joseph with the same close familiarity, respect and high honor which, as a Son of His Father, He gave him when He walked among men, or rather, that he fulfills and perfects this relationship. The joy of Eternal happiness enters into man's heart; but the Lord preferred to say to Joseph "Enter thou into joy" that he might mystically signify to him joy which should not only be within him, but everywhere about him, absorbing his whole being and swallowing him up in an infinite depth of joy . . .

Therefore remember us, blessed Joseph, and by the voice of your prayers, intercede with Him who was believed to be your Son; and direct toward us the compassion of the Blessed Virgin, your Bride and the Mother of Him who, with the Father and the Holy Spirit, lives and reigns for ever and ever. Amen.

Reflecting upon the happy death of St. Joseph, attended by everything that is greatest in Heaven and on earth, Bernardine felt at a loss to express the Heavenly consolation and delights which filled this most Blessed of all souls after that of Mary.

St. Bernardine felt that St. Joseph was one of the risen. Furthermore, he says that Christ crowned His foster-father with the same privilege which he bestowed on His Mother; that as He assumed Her into

Heaven body and soul, He also took up Joseph with Him in the glory of the Resurrection. That as Jesus, Mary and Joseph had lived together on earth, they now reign in Heaven in glory of Body and Soul.

He says that St. Joseph had in his hands the keys to open the gates of the New Law and to close those of the Law of Moses.

Mary, as the Daughter of the Eternal Father, had been endowed with incalculable treasures of grace. Bernardine was of the opinion that these, so far as he is capable of being their recipient, were communicated to Joseph when the Blessed Virgin, accepting him as Her spouse, gave him Her heart.

According to St. Bernardine, there was reason for keeping St. Joseph in the background and almost hidden fearing the amplification of his cultus might furnish a pretext to the heretics to assert that he was not the reputed father but the natural father of our Divine Lord. It is for this reason that care was taken in those days to add "putative" to his title of father, a precaution the Evangelist, St. Luke did not take, neither did our Lady Herself.

St. Joseph being entirely at the service of Jesus, St. Bernardine proposed that we think of the luminous faith that inspired Joseph as he tended the tiny body of the Christ Child, and of the rapt attention with which he later followed every movement and every word of the Boy. He would stop in utter amazement at the thought that the Son of God had become his Son and chosen him to feed and guide and protect Him during His mortal life.

When looking at the characteristics of St. Joseph's Adoration, St. Bernardine gave this thought. Who can deny that during His childhood and youth Christ imprinted intangible impressions of His divinity in Joseph and filled him with indescribable delights, as

Joseph held Him in his arms and talked with Him or as the Child mouthed His first stumbling words? Christ's grace overflowed into Joseph's soul through various outward expressions — a tender glance, a baby smile, a casual word, or a warm embrace. Yes, what sweet embraces Joseph received from Him! And what a thrill of joy at the sound of the baby voice calling him father! He would hold the Child tenderly on his heart and his burning love would fuse the two into one.

God has bestowed upon St. Joseph a special mission in the Church. Compare Joseph with the whole Church. Is he not the chosen one who enabled Christ to enter into the world according to the Laws of order and fitness? Through Mary, the Church was made worthy to receive Christ, and therefore the Church is indebted to Her. Next to that, the Church owes Her greatest debt of gratitude and veneration to St. Joseph, for he is the Key to the Old Testament. It is by him that the Patriarchs and the Prophets reaped the fruit of God's promise. Alone among them all, Joseph saw with his own eyes and possessed the Redeemer promised to the rest of men.

We can well say, therefore, that St. Joseph was prefigured by the patriarch Joseph, who kept supplies of wheat for his people. But how much greater than his prototype was St. Joseph. The old Joseph gave the Egyptians mere bread for their bodies. St. Joseph nourished and with tenderest care preserved for the elect of all ages Him Who is the Bread of Heaven and gives Eternal Life.

Bernardine of Siena tells us that if the Church is indebted to Mary for receiving Christ worthily, it is also indebted to Joseph for possessing Christ bodily, a grace which was his exclusive privilege. His book "Sermon on St. Joseph" was a major influence to stimulate the Devotion to St. Joseph in different parts of Italy.

John Gerson

John Cardinal Gerson (born 1363; died in Lyons 1429) was noted as the great Doctor and Theologian for the devotion to St. Joseph. John Gerson delivered a sermon at the Council of Constance on September 8, 1416. The following are excerpts from his sermon.

Joseph was the physical father of Jesus in the eyes of men. He was father by his solicitude as fosterer and he was father through generation. It is true that he did not himself beget Jesus, but his wife Mary did so by the operation of the Holy Spirit, who in a sense took the place of Joseph, not through a physical but through a mysterious spiritual generation. Joseph, therefore, can be called, not indeed the natural father of Jesus, but the legal father, to whom the Holy Spirit had given generative powers that were more efficacious than those that are natural. . . .

Let us with religious devotion consider this: by the natural bond that unites a family, the Son, Jesus is beholden to His Mother, the Mother to Her husband and both Son and Mother to Joseph as guardian and provider. And he was the head of Mary and so had a measure of authority over Her just as She, by right of natural motherhood, had over Her son, Jesus. . . . Jesus spoke truly when He said, "Where I am there also shall My servant be" (John 12:26), surely he who, after Mary, was closest to Him on Earth, who was so dutiful and faithful in his service of Him, must have a place nearest to Him in Heaven.

While addressing the Council, Cardinal Gerson was seeking the intercession of St. Joseph to bring about unity in the Church which was facing disasters due to the activities of all heretics. . . .

Gerson started the campaign for the introduction of a feast of St. Joseph in the liturgy of the Church. He insisted that the "Feast of the Espousal of Joseph and Mary" was to be celebrated with a votive mass. During the Council of Constance he reiterated his demand for instituting the Feast of St. Joseph and to honor him as the patron of the Universal Church.[7] Since the Council was very busy with other urgent matters, it could not take up Gerson's suggestions for implementation although it had a favorable inclination to do so. However, it is to be noted with gratification that his sermon had a propaganda value among the prelates of various countries who attended the Council, since they started to lay out plans to honor St. Joseph with great vigor in the liturgy.

Pierre d'Ailly

Pierre d'Ailly (born 1350 in Compiegne, died probably 1420 in Avignon), Cardinal of Cambrai, Gerson's celebrated master, wrote that St. Joseph must be highly glorified, for he had greatly humbled himself. For many years, our holy Patriarch had been hidden in his profound humility, like a candle under a basket, and had loved to remain so. But the time had come when he who humbled himself was to be exalted, and be exalted in proportion to his humility. He was now to become the light set upon its candlestick to illuminate the whole Church with its beneficent rays.

As a result of Cardinal Gerson's sermon at the Council of Constance, Cardinal D'Ailly published his *Treatise on St. Joseph.* In this work he enumerated twelve honors of St. Joseph based on the Gospels of Matthew and Luke. This book surpassed the writings of Gerson. Many extracts were taken from his Treatise and used as Offices of the various local Feasts in honor of our dear saint. Therefore indirectly Pierre D'Ailly influenced the Liturgy of the Feast of St. Joseph. His purpose was to introduce a special feast in honor of St. Joseph. The most important among the honors the

Cardinal brought out were: (1) Joseph's royal ancestry to the house of David. (2) His true marriage of our Lady. (3) His virginity. (4) His call to the service of Mary and Jesus. (5) His initiation into the Divine mysteries. (6) His Justice through faith. (7) His naming the Divine Child. (8) His presence at the great mysteries of faith. (9) The prophecy of Simeon and Anna at the temple. (10) His close association with Jesus and Mary. (11) The obedience of the Child Jesus to him. (12) His physical effort to feed and nourish the Divine child and to maintain the family.

We now come to the end of the Middle Ages marked by the downfall of Rome c.476 to the Renaissance in 1450. History records that with the convocation of the Council of Basel in 1431, another in a long series of attacks were placed upon the authority of the Pope. Now with the Renaissance, which may have actually begun with Dante in the early 1300's, was a period of great revival of art, literature and learning in Europe, extending into the 16th century. It began in Italy and spread gradually to other countries marking the transition from the Medieval world to the Modern. At this time the Saints ceased to be hieratic and became patrons for a trade or a specific cause. While mothers were venerating St. Anne, St. Joseph still remained in the background, still overshadowed.

---

6 and 7 Not to be officially declared until 1870.

CHAPTER FOUR

Now we enter the mid 15th Century, where turmoil has abounded in the Church, St. Joseph's devotion continues to grow, yet there is still much to be accomplished.

Bernardine de Bustis

Bernardine de Bustis makes this bold assertion: "Since Joseph was to be guardian, companion and ruler of the most Blessed Virgin and of the Child Jesus, is it possible to conceive that God could have made a mistake in the choice of him? Or that He could have permitted him to be deficient in any respect? Or could have failed to make him most perfect? The very idea would be the grossest of errors. When God selects anyone to perform some great work He bestows upon him every virtue needed for its accomplishment"...

Bernardine expressed the sentiment that whatever Joseph might ask for us of Jesus and Mary, it was impossible that he could meet with a refusal.

Schism of the East

The final separation between the East and the West took place in 1472. This is called the Schism of the East. Unfortunately the Orthodox Eastern Church and the Roman Catholic Church have remained separated to this day.

Pope Sixtus IV

Pope Sixtus IV introduced St. Joseph's feast day into the calendar of the Church of Rome in 1479. He also wished the feast to be inserted in the Roman Missal and the Breviary as a feast to be celebrated in Rome. In 1480, other Italian dioceses followed the example

"Marriage of the Virgin" by Raphael

of Rome in the celebration of St. Joseph's feast.

The early 1500's were characterized by the discovery of Mexico, United States of America from Florida to lower California and Canada. Few perhaps are aware of the extraordinary devotion to St. Joseph throughout the continent of America. "On conquest of this New World, the first Fathers planted devotion to St. Joseph with the true faith." And what was true of Spanish America was also true of the French Canadian Missions, and wherever the Gospel was preached to the Indians of North America.

Raphael

Raphael was an Italian painter during the Renaissance. To the great number of later paintings which represent St. Joseph as an old man there is this one notable exception. Raphael painted *Sposalizio* or *Marriage of the Virgin* during the period 1500–1504 in Perugia. It is justly famous. The artist in his genius and sound instinct has saved St. Joseph from the blunder of belittling the bridegroom. In the picture there is only one person of advanced age, only one person with a venerable white beard, and it is not St. Joseph, but the High Priest. St. Joseph is shown with the short crisp beard of a man in the prime of his life.

In 1508 the Dominican chapter at Rome ruled that the Feast of St. Joseph should continue according to the local custom and it should be ranked among the extraordinary feasts of the order. Later, in 1522 it was made obligatory in the Dominican missals and breviaries.

With the reduction of clergymen caused by the Black Death, the diminished prestige of the Papacy because of the exile in Avignon and the Schism of the

West, and the fact that all countries were largely pervaded by anticlerical sentiment and by doctrines subversive of ecclesiastical authority, there was a general assault upon the doctrine and policy of the Church which contributed to the Reformation. There had been concurrently a relaxation of religious doctrine, a neglect for the sacraments and a general luxury of life stemming from the secular spirit of the Renaissance. All this led to the beginning of the Reformation as started by Martin Luther, an Augustinian monk, who disapproved of the manner in which Pope Leo X attempted to raise funds for the reconstruction of St. Peter's Basilica in Rome. Thus, on October 31, 1517, Luther nailed his 95 Theses on the door of Castle Church in Wittenburg, which was the beginning of the Reformation. The purpose was to reform the Roman Catholic Church, however, the result was the establishment of Protestant Churches.

Isidore de Isolano

Isidore de Isolano, a Dominican priest, said: "The Holy Spirit will not rest from inciting the hearts of the faithful until the Universal Church honors with ecstasy the divine Joseph with a new veneration, founds monasteries, builds churches, erects altars in his name, multiplies his feasts and celebrates them more solemnly.

As early as 1522, Isolano wrote "the hidden merits of Joseph shall be by degrees unveiled and made manifest to the whole world, and an inexhaustible treasure will be revealed. The Vicar of Christ upon Earth will command the feasts of the reputed father of Jesus and spouse of the Queen of the World to be celebrated to the utmost boundaries of the kingdom of the Church Militant. In the calendar of the saints the name of Joseph shall be sung at the head, not in the rear. Even as in Heaven he was ever above, so on earth he shall not be below."

Isolano was one of the first opponents of Martin Luther. He wrote the first great treatise devoted to St. Joseph, published in 1522, called *A Summa of the Gifts of St. Joseph.* It was dedicated to Pope Alban VI, who the author implored to institute a feast of St. Joseph for the whole church. Some of the ideas mentioned, are notably, that St. Joseph was sanctified in his mother's womb. He is presented as being man's most powerful intercessor after the Blessed Virgin.

Isadore tells us before the day of Judgement, all people will come to know and adore the name of the Lord, and praise the Lord for the great gifts He Himself placed in St. Joseph whom he had left in obscurity throughout a long period. Therefore the fame of St. Joseph will overflow with the gifts of all goods of the earth. Great men will search on the inner gifts of God that are hidden in St. Joseph. Thus according to Isidor, "Joseph who is overall in heaven, will no longer be disregarded on earth."

Bernardine of Laredo

Bernardine of Laredo (1482–1540) was a Franciscan lay brother whose works influenced St. Teresa. Bernardine was against the general opinion of Joseph's advanced age. He explains the erroneous opinion by pointing out that in the early Church there were heretics who claimed that Joseph was the natural father of Jesus. By way of refuting this heresy, paintings began to show "St. Joseph as an old man." But to continue doing this after the heresy had been disposed of — he says — "is quite silly."

St. Teresa of Jesus

St. Teresa of Jesus was born in 1515 at Avila in Old Castille. She was foundress of the religious order of

Discalced or Barefoot Carmelites. St. Teresa joined the Carmelite Order in 1535. Long troubled by relaxed discipline into which some communities had lapsed, she was determined to devote herself to the reform of the order. Through Papal intervention in her behalf, she overcame the bitter opposition of her immediate ecclesiastical superiors and in 1562 succeeded in founding at Avila, the convent of St. Joseph, the first community of Reformed or Discalced Carmelite Nuns. In 1567 she was given permission to found similar orders for men. St. Teresa could be called St. Joseph's personal saint with reference to her diligence in spreading his devotion.

She took him as her special patron and protector. When she joined the Carmelite Order, she was imbued with this devotion, which is said to be the Order's inheritance. She ardently exerted herself for its propagation. Many who had not given much attention to the efforts made in the previous century, particularly to those of the learned and devout Chancellor, Gerson, have attributed its revival solely to her influence. It is true indeed, that none contributed so effectively as did St. Teresa to make the love of St. Joseph take possession of the hearts of the great body of the faithful. In this we may possibly see a special Divine dispensation.

During an illness in which no earthly physician was able to give her relief, St. Teresa decided to implore the Blessed in Heaven to restore her health. She writes: "I chose for my patron and lord the glorious St. Joseph, and I recommend myself earnestly to him. I saw that, both from my present trouble, and from those of greater consequence relating to my honor and the loss of my soul, my Father and Lord delivered me and rendered me greater services than I knew how to ask for. *I do not remember that I ever asked him at any time for anything which he did not obtain for me.* It fills me with amazement when I consider the numberless graces which God has granted me through the intercession of this Blessed saint and the perils, both of body and soul, from which he has delivered me."

To other saints the most high seems to have given grace to succor men in some special necessity, but this glorious saint, I know by experience, has the power to help us in *all.* Our Lord wishes us to understand by this, as He Himself was subject to St. Joseph while on Earth, recognizing in him the authority of foster-father and guardian, so now in Heaven He is pleased to grant all his requests. Knowing by experience St. Joseph's astonishing influence with God, I would wish to persuade everyone to honor him with particular devotion. I have always seen those who honored him in a special manner make progress in virtue, for this Heavenly protector favors in a striking manner the spiritual advancement of souls who commend themselves to him. For several years I have been accustomed to ask some favor on his feast, and I have always received it. If the petition was in any way amiss, he directs it aright for my greater welfare. If anyone does not believe it, I beg of him, for the love of God, to make the trial. He will see by experience, how advantageous it is to commend himself to this glorious saint and to honor him with particular devotion. *"Those who are devoted to prayer should, in a special manner, cherish devotion to St. Joseph."*

Our Blessed Lady appeared to St. Teresa, when in an ecstasy, and after bestowing on her the most loving caresses, clothed her in a robe of beautiful whiteness, and with Her own hands put a golden collar and cross round her neck, in recompense of the honor which she had procured for St. Joseph. On several other occasions She magnificently rewarded the saint for her devotion to Her spouse.

St. Teresa organized the new branch of the old order, with the aid of St. John of the Cross (1542–91), the Spanish Mystic and Doctor of the Church. In 1580 the Discalced Carmelites received Papal recognition as an independent monastic body. St. Teresa died in 1582, was cannonized in 1622 and in 1970 she was proclaimed a Doctor of the Church, the first woman to be so named.

Council of Trent

The fight over the authority of the Papacy has continued. Finally during the Council of Trent, the papacy reconstituted itself in adjustment to the Reformation. Pope Pius IV, during the Council of Trent (1545–1563), requested St. Joseph to be included in the Church Calendar of the Saints.

The Benedictines uniformly accepted the Feast of St. Joseph after the Council of Trent.

Francisco Suarez

Francisco Suarez (1548–1617) was a Spanish Jesuit who says "I will not neglect to call attention to the rather general belief that this saint gloriously reigns with Christ in soul and body. Since he died before Christ, it is very likely that he was one of those who arose at the time of the death or resurrection of Christ and who — as many believe — passed on to the immortal life in the soul and body."

St. Lawrence of Brindisi

St. Lawrence of Brindisi (July 22, 1559 – July 22, 1619) said Joseph was predestined like Jesus and Mary before the Angels. By predestination of Joseph, Lawrence means, that God prepared him with grace and glory, holiness and happiness before his Birth. Lawrence held that Joseph was predestined to a greater glory in heaven like Mary above the Angels and saints and therefore his holiness in this world surpassed even that of the Angels in heaven.

Brother Alexis

It was on March 19th, 1581, the anniversary of St. Joseph's transit from Earth, when feeling death to be approaching, Brother Alexis, a Capuchin lay brother with great devotion to St. Joseph, collected what little remaining strength he possessed, to beg the religious; his brethren, who were assisting him, to light some candles, since St. Joseph was coming to him. They did so, and very soon the dying man exclaimed: "Here is the Queen of Heaven and St. Joseph! Kneel down, O fathers, and give a worthy reception." As he said this he expired.

Folk Literature

Side by side with the growth of theological literature, there was another literature that grew up and became very popular among the common folk known as "folk stories". The life of Mary was depicted in prose and poetry with innumerable tales attached to it in these folk stories. Such folk stories exercised tremendous influence to stimulate the growth of the devotion to St. Joseph because the veneration of our Lady and the veneration of St. Joseph went hand in hand.

CHAPTER FIVE

Francis de Sales

The 17th Century affords us the privilege of meeting Francis de Sales (1567–1622). St. Francis de Sales was the great Missioner and teacher for the cultus of St. Joseph. It was he who said, "St. Joseph is in Heaven in body and in soul, of that there is no doubt."

In a sermon on the Feast of St. Joseph, St. Francis says: 'The just shall flourish like the palm tree.' (Ps. 91:13) This being presupposed, I will introduce my subject by observing that the palm tree, among a great number of peculiar properties, has three special ones, which also belong in a remarkable manner to the saint whose feast we are keeping. That saint, who is recorded by the Church, being like the *palm tree.* He is compared to the palm, which is the king of trees, and which has the properties of virginity, humility, courage and constancy, all virtues which the glorious St. Joseph excelled so greatly. If comparisons were made, many would maintain that he surpasses all other saints in these three virtues.

He continues: God having destined from all eternity, in his Divine Providence, that a 'Virgin should conceive a Son' (Is: 7:14), who should be both God and man, willed nevertheless that this Virgin should be married. 'But, O God!' exclaim the Holy Doctors, 'for what reason did thou ordain two things so different, to be a Virgin and Bride at the same time?' . . . Therefore, in order to shield and protect this purity and virginity, it was necessary that God's Plan should commit Her to the guardianship of a man absolutely pure, and that this Virgin should conceive and bring forth this sweet *Fruit* (Cant 2:3) of life, our Lord, under the shadow of Holy Marriage. St. Joseph, then, was like a palm tree which, though bearing no fruit, is yet not unfruitful, but has a great share in the fruit of the female palm. Not that St. Joseph contributed anything towards that Holy and Glorious Fruit, except indeed the shadow of marriage, which prevented our Lady from being exposed to those calumnies and censures which the signs of her approaching motherhood would have brought upon her...

When speaking on St. Joseph's virtue of obedience, St. Francis said "when the angel ordered Joseph to take the Mother and Child and flee into Egypt until he should tell him to return, he was sparing in his words, treating Joseph like a true religious. "Go and do not come back until I tell you." We learn from the conciseness and simplicity of their conversation how we must embark on the sea of Divine Providence without food, without rudder or sail, in a word, without any provisions, leaving the success of our affairs to the Lord, without a worry or a fear for the future.

Poor Saint Joseph could well have objected, "Must I leave immediately? If I am to take the Mother and Child, tell me, if you can, how I will find food for them on the Journey? For you know that we have no money." But he says nothing; he confides entirely in God's foresight to help him obtain their meager sustenance either from his trade or from the alms they will receive. Certainly the first religious were remarkable for their confidence in God to provide for their needs; they left all care of themselves in the hands of Divine Providence.

I think it is necessary to leave in the hands of Divine Providence the care of our spiritual life and of our perfection; for it is nothing else than our excessive solicitude for ourselves that makes us lose our peace of mind and puts us into strange and changeable moods. When we commit a fault, however small it be, we think everything is lost; is it any wonder that we fail at times? But I am so often troubled with dryness that I feel that I am not close to God, who is so full of consolations. We must be like St. Joseph, calm in our trials and leave it to our Lord to free us from them when it pleases him to do so.

What was his poverty like? It was that disdained poverty which made him a destitute outcast. The voluntary poverty practiced by religious is quite mild, especially since it allows them the necessities of life and deprives them only of superfluous needs. But the poverty of St. Joseph, of our Lord, and of Mary was not like that. Though it was voluntary and dear to them, it was none the less a severe poverty. Everyone thought of this great Saint as a poor carpenter, who, though he worked with unequalled love to support his little family, was doubtless unable to give them many of the necessities of life. When he had done his best, he humbly submitted to the will of God and went on in poverty and humiliation, never allowing himself to be dismayed or overcome by the frequent attacks of the devil.

Who can doubt that Mary was more worthy than St. Joseph, had more discretion and more of the qualities essential to one in authority? Yet the angel told her nothing at all about preparations for the flight, about leaving, returning, or anything else. Does it not seem that the angel was greatly mistaken in addressing himself to Joseph rather than to Mary who, because she bore the Treasure of the Eternal Father, was the mistress of the house? She could have said to her husband: "Why should I go to Egypt? My son has not revealed to me that I should go, nor has the angel spoken to me about it."

But our Lady said nothing of the kind; she was not offended at the angel's dealing with Joseph. She obeyed simply and humbly.

These are the virtues that will enable us to triumph over our adversaries in this life, and to merit the grace of enjoying in the life to come the reward prepared for those who follow the example St. Joseph gave them on earth.

Jean de Bolland

Jean de Bolland (1596–1665) was a Flemish Jesuit Hagiologist, which means a recorder of the lives of saints. He was the first editor of the first volumes of the collection *Acta Sanctorum*. His followers became known as Bollandists. They reaffirm the record of more than 20,000 saints.

The Bollandists maintained that the now empty tomb of Joseph was in the Valley of Josaphat. This theory prevails to present day.

By their predecessors testimony, "St. Joseph by his purity surpassed all the angels of Heaven, even the highest of them." The Bollandists, famous Catholic writers in the lives of the saints, state that the whole Latin Church, after St. Jerome, held that St. Joseph lived and died a virgin.

The Peace of Westphalia in 1648 brought an end to the Thirty Years War. This series of European Wars were on political and religious issues. Originally the fight was between the German Catholics and the German Protestants, but later expanded involving the Swedish, French and Spanish. With the end of the Thirty Years War, the emergence for the Modern Church is in place.

Venerable Mary of Agreda

Venerable Mary of Jesus of Agreda (April 2, 1602–May 24, 1665) was a Poor Clare mystical writer.

The Blessed Virgin spoke to Venerable Mary saying: "My daughter, although you have written that my spouse, Joseph, was one of the greatest saints and most noble princes of the Celestial Jerusalem, you cannot now declare his eminent sanctity. Mortals can never know it until they enjoy the vision of God, in which they will, with admiration, discover the mystery, and they will praise the Lord for it. In the last day when all men will be judged, the unhappy damned will weep bitterly for not having known, because of their sins, this powerful and efficacious means for their salvation, and for not having availed themselves of it, as they could have done, to recover the grace of the last judge.

The world has been greatly ignorant of the magnitude of the prerogatives which the Supreme Lord has accorded my holy spouse. And how powerful is his intercession with His Divine Majesty. Be assured that he is one of the greatest favorites of God, and one of the most capable of appeasing His justice against sinners. I desire you to be most grateful to the goodness of the Lord for the favor which I have granted to you on this occasion, and that you will render Him continual thanks for the illumination that you have received touching this mystery. Endeavor also, in the future, to augment your devotion for my holy spouse, and bless the Lord for He has favored him with so much liberality, and also for the consolation that I enjoyed in bearing him company and knowing his perfections.

"You must avail yourself of his intercession in all your necessities, and so act to multiply the numbers of his votaries. Recommend to your daughters to distinguish themselves in this devotion, since the Most High grants on Earth that which My spouse requests in Heaven. And he will unite to these requests extraordinary favors for men, provided they do not render themselves unworthy to receive them."

"All these privileges respond to the perfection, the innocence, and to the eminent virtues of this admirable saint, because they have attracted the complaisance of the Lord, Who destines for him inconceivable largesses, and who desires to show great mercy to those who will have recourse to his intercession."

To this pious servant of God, it was revealed that choirs of angels assisted at the death of St. Joseph, singing hymns of Heavenly joy.

In her book of revelations, "La Mistica Ciudad de Dios" (The Mystic City of God), she popularized the idea that St. Joseph was thirty years old when he married Mary. She also said, "St. Joseph was sanctified in the Mother's womb."

As she has told us, St. Joseph consecrated himself to God very early in his youth and made a vow of virginity which he kept all through life. For if he did not practice chastity all his life he would have been of no value as a moral virtue. Moreover, the Gospel calls St. Joseph "a just man", which means that he possessed all the virtues and this would not be true if he lacked the virtue of chastity. Indeed, it is precisely because he possessed this virtue that he had all the other virtues which are the companions and servants of chastity. Humility, modesty, recollection, obedience, mortification, lively faith, firm hope, ardent charity, all wait upon chastity as their mistress. For he who practices chastity exercises also all the other Christian virtues.

Jacques-Benigne Bossuet

Jacques-Benigne Bossuet (1627–1704), a French bishop and orator, wrote two sermons devoted to St. Joseph and are among the finest ever written in his praise. He expounds on the saint's virtues in detail, his humility, his purity, his faith that surpassed the faith of Abraham. He stresses the virginal character of the marriage with Mary. He examines Joseph's spiritual fatherhood with respect to the Son of God. He compares St. Joseph with the Apostles, but without trying to give him preeminence over them. Their vocations were different. The Apostles were chosen to reveal the Son of God, but Joseph was called to hide Him. Joseph's true greatness lies in his hidden life.

In Fr. Bossuet's first panegyric on St. Joseph he expounds: If there has ever been a trust that deserved to be called holy and to be looked after with a holy care, it is the one which the Providence of the Eternal Father committed to righteous Joseph. I see his house as a temple, where God chooses to dwell and to be left there in trust; and Joseph had to be dedicated to take charge of this Sacred Treasure. And so he was. His body was consecrated by continence, and his soul by every gift grace can bestow. . . .

Fr. Bossuet continues, I do not propose to base my praises of St. Joseph on any dubious surmises, but on solid doctrine drawn from the Divine Scriptures and from the Fathers, their faithful exponents. . . . Let me show you this great saint whom God chose among all others to receive charge of His Treasure and to be His trustee on this earth. . . . The name of trustee is a sign of esteem and an indication of a man's integrity. When we are going to entrust something to somebody, we choose one of our friends whose virtue is best recognized, whose fidelity is most reliable, whom we know intimately and trust thoroughly. God made him trustee, not simply of Blessed Mary, but also of His Son. . . .

The first of his trusts was Mary's holy virginity, which Joseph kept under the sacred cover of marriage. . . . The second was Jesus Christ, whom the Heavenly

Father put into his hands that he might be as a father to the Holy Child, Who could have no earthly father. A third, we must assume that a secret is a trust and Joseph is trustee of the Eternal Father, because He has told him His secret. What secret, you ask? The wondrous taking by His Son of human flesh.

It was God's will not to reveal Jesus Christ to the world until His hour had come.... The Eternal Father, revealed the mystery to St. Joseph in secret and under obligation of silence....

For Joseph to safeguard Mary's virginity under cover of marriage, it was needful that he should be pure as an angel, so that his virtue could in some sort, correspond to the purity of his maiden bride. To protect the Savior, amid the dangers of His childhood, it was necessary that Joseph be immovably faithful, a faith that could not be shaken by threat of adversity that Joseph should be specially humble, avoiding the public gaze, withholding himself from the world, loving to be hidden with Christ Jesus.... Virginity was necessary for the bringing of Jesus Christ into the world.

The doctors of old define Christian virginity, with one voice that it is an emulation of the life of angels. That it raises men above the body by a rejection of its delights, and that it so exalts the flesh that in a way it equals, the purity of spirit. I appeal to the great Augustine to tell us in a sentence what he thinks of virgins. "They already have in the flesh something that is not of the flesh." You see, then, that according to this father of the Church virginity is like a mean between spirit and body, and brings us nearer to spiritual natures. Hence it can easily be perceived how this virtue advances the mystery of the Incarnation. It is the closest union of God and man, of the Godhead with human flesh. "The Word was made flesh" said the evangelist St. John. There you have the union, and there you have the mystery.

The godhead of the Eternal Word, willing to take to Himself a mortal body, chose holy virginity as the blessed go-between. Having something spiritual about it, it was able in a certain sense to prepare flesh to be united with pure spirit. . . . It is through virginity that God agrees to come and live among men. . . .

I am not afraid to affirm that Joseph had a part in this great miracle. For if an angelic purity is the good of holy Mary, it is the trust of righteous Joseph. . . . Mary dedicated fruitful virginity, Joseph safeguarded it, and together they offered it to the eternal Father as a good looked after by their common efforts. . . . Because of that faithful wedlock, they both are entitled to be called Christ's parents. What a mystery of purity! What a blessed fatherhood! What imperishable light shines through the whole of this marriage!

That Joseph should be the protector of Mary's fruitful virginity was not enough. The Eternal Father decreed a yet higher destiny and confided Jesus Christ Himself to his care. . . . Joseph was the chosen one for this ministry. Joseph accepted this trust and how he put all his heart and soul into being a father to the orphan. From then on he lived only for Jesus, all his concern was for Him. He had a father's heart for Him, and what he was not by nature he became by love.

The same Divine hand that fashions each man's heart gave a father's heart to Joseph and a son's heart to Jesus, so that Jesus obeyed Joseph and Joseph did not fear to command Jesus. . . . God had chosen Joseph to act as father to His Son in this world. God had charged Joseph's breast with some ray or spark of His own boundless love for His Son. . . . Wherever Jesus comes He brings His cross, He brings the thorns, and all whom He loves must share them. Joseph and Mary were poor. But they had never been homeless. They had somewhere to go. But when this Child comes into the world there is no room for them, and they have to find refuge in a stable. . . . Joseph counted himself happy to suffer in Jesus' company. He was disturbed in mind, but the whole reason for his alarm was the danger overhanging the Divine Child, Who was more dear to him than life itself.

He is revealed to the Apostles in order that they may preach Him throughout the world. He is revealed to Joseph in order that he may hide Him and keep silent about Him. . . . He who glorifies the Apostles in the renown of their preaching glorifies St. Joseph in the humility of his silence. And from that we have to learn that the glory of Christians lies, not in distinguished achievements and offices, but in doing what God wills. The life of sinners generally makes more noise than the life of the righteous, for selfishness and insurgent passions create disturbance all over the world. . . .

Universal Recognition

Pope Gregory XV made St. Joseph's feast day a part of the calendar of the Universal Church, on May 8, 1621. This declaration became a Holyday of Obligation throughout the world.

A General Chapter was held in 1621 where the glorious St. Joseph was unanimously chosen as the patron or father of the whole Reformed Order of the Carmelites.

In 1624 St. Joseph was declared Patron Saint of Canada.

The second half of the 17th century witnessed the phenomenal growth of devotion to St. Joseph mainly in the Catholic countries of Europe. Leopold I of

Austria, son of Ferdinand III sought the intercession of St. Joseph to obtain a male child as his successor. When he got the child he was named Joseph to manifest his gratitude to St. Joseph, and a public declaration was made making St. Joseph the patron of Austria. During his regime Austria was menaced by the Turkish invasion. In 1683 the Turks were defeated at Vienna by seeking the aid of St. Joseph, and Leopold acknowledged this fact by writing Pope Innocent XI requesting the favor of the Pope to stimulate the growth of the devotion towards St. Joseph by including first the name of St. Joseph in the Litany of all saints and secondly, by permitting the Feast of the Patronage of St. Joseph to be celebrated on the third Sunday after Easter.

Devotion to St. Joseph in Spain was very praiseworthy. Charles II requested the Pope to declare St. Joseph patron of Spain. In Germany, Bishop Bernard Von Galen received Papal permission to dedicate his diocese to St. Joseph and the clergy of the diocese were asked to spread the love and knowledge of St. Joseph among the faithful and thereby to increase their devotion towards the saint especially to obtain his powerful intercession for a happy death. France followed the same. They wished to further the cultus of St. Joseph, especially through the work of Fr. Pierre Cotton, S.J. in the church of Lyons. In Paris, the Cistercians dedicated their church to St. Joseph. Progress is being made.

Pope Clement X, on December 6, 1670, accorded to the Feast of St. Joseph the rite of a double of the second class. This was already being celebrated in many places by a special indult of the Holy See.

A rite of a double of the second class would be a Holyday of Obligation only preempted by the Sundays of Advent, Lent and Pentecost, specifically those of a rite of a double of the first class. This now gave St. Joseph the honor many of the Doctors of the Church had longed for.

On August 17, 1678, Pope Innocent XI confirmed, in an Apostolic Brief, St. Joseph as Patron and Protector of the Chinese Missions. In 1679, He declared St. Joseph Patron Saint of Spain.

Due to factional nationalistic resentment to the decree of St. Joseph as Patron Saint of Spain, the decree of 1679 was reversed in 1680.

After the Carmelite's choice in 1621 of St. Joseph as their Patron, an office was composed for St. Joseph in 1689. With the Church's approbation, the Feast began to be celebrated under the title of the Patronage of St. Joseph on the Third Sunday after Easter.

St. Leonard of Port Maurice

St. Leonard of Port Maurice (1676–1751), in proclaiming the eulogium of St. Francis de Sales, exclaims that Joseph was transported in body and in soul to the empyrean by a particular privilege, which appears to be indicated in the Proverbs, where it is said that all of Her (Mary's) household are "clothed with double garments," which interpreters have understood as signifying the twofold glorification of soul and body.

CHAPTER SIX

St. Alphonsus Liguori

The 18th Century commences with the introduction to St. Alphonsus Liguori (1696–1787). In 1732 he founded The Missionary Congregation of Liguorians or Redemptorists in order to spread religion among the poor. "The holy example of Jesus Christ, Who, while upon earth, honored St. Joseph so highly and was obedient to him during His life," should be sufficient to inflame the hearts of all with devotion to this saint.

Since we all must die, we should cherish a special devotion to St. Joseph that he may obtain for us a Happy Death. All Christians regard him as the advocate of the dying, who assists at the hour of death those who honored him during their life. He further gives these three reasons: First, because Jesus Christ loved him not only as a friend but as a father, and on this account his mediation is far more efficacious than that of any other saint. Second, because St. Joseph has ordained special power against the evil spirits. Especially those who tempt us with redoubled vigor at the hour of death. Third, the assistance given St. Joseph at his death by Jesus and Mary obtained for him the right to secure a holy and peaceful death for his servants. Hence, if they invoke him at the hour of death he will not only help them, but he will also obtain for them the assistance of Jesus and Mary. We must be convinced that God will not refuse St. Joseph any grace he asks for those who honor him.

St. Alphonsus gives this thought on the devotedness of St. Joseph. God did not choose Joseph only to be Mary's strength amid the trials of their exile, nor even to be just the foster-father of Jesus. He wanted Joseph to be a cooperator in the Redemption of the world, the work which belonged properly to the three Divine Persons. Since God wanted Joseph to hold the place of father toward Jesus, He confided to him the care of nourishing the Child and defending him against the wiles of the enemy. "Take the Child," He says as if quoting the words of the Psalms: "to you has been given the care of the poor." Yes, Joseph, I have sent My Son on earth poor, humble, without riches or honors. He shall be despised and called the son of a carpenter because of your common trade. I wanted you to be poor, because I destined you to be the fosterfather of My Son who is also poor. For He has not come into the world to govern, but to save men by His sufferings and death. He will be persecuted and you will share His sufferings. Watch over Him and be faithful to Me.

The following are excerpts from a sermon given in Naples in 1771:

We indeed ought to honor St. Joseph, seeing that the Son of God Himself was pleased to honor him by calling him father. "Christ," says Origen, "gave to Joseph the honor due to a parent." St. Alphonsus continues, since, the King of kings was pleased to raise him to such a height, it is right, and our duty, to try to honor Joseph as much as we can.... "What angel or saint," asks St. Basil, "ever deserved to be called the father of the Son of God? Joseph alone was thus called.".... As Alphonsus says, Joseph gave orders in that household, and the Son of God obeyed. He was subject to His parents. "This subjection," says Gerson, "shows the humbleness of Jesus Christ. It also shows the high place of Joseph. To what greater height can a man be raised than to have a father's authority over Him who commands kings?"

St. Alphonsus tells us St. Bernard calls St. Joseph

"a wise and faithful servant, whom the Lord made the comfort of His mother, the nourisher of His manhood, the sole and faithful coadjutor on earth of the great council."

God gave Joseph a father's love, care and authority over Jesus. His was a father's affection, that he might watch over Him with great love. His was a father's responsibility, that he might take great care of Him. His was a father's authority, that he might be sure he would be obeyed in all that he decided for his son. . . . God willed that St. Joseph should be present at Jesus' birth so that he might be a faithful witness of the glory given by the angels to God at Bethlehem. A witness, too, of what was revealed to the shepherds, who, when they came to visit the Savior that had been foretold to them, related all to Mary and Joseph. A witness, again, to the coming of the Magi who, guided by a star, had traveled from afar to worship the Holy Child, as they themselves declared. God also willed that Joseph should join with Mary in dedicating the newborn babe then offered Him up to die for the salvation of the world according to the Scriptures, in which the passion of Christ had been foretold, as was well known to them both.

God endowed him with all the gifts of wisdom and holiness called for by such a trust. Nor can we doubt that He endowed him with all the graces and privileges granted to other saints. Among these gifts, says Gerson and Suarez, were three special ones. Namely, that Joseph was sanctified in his mother's womb, like Jeremiah and John the Baptist. That he was at the same time confirmed in grace, and that he was always free from inordinate impulses. By the merit of his own purity, St. Joseph obtains the grace of deliverance from fleshly inclinations for those who devoutly ask for his intercession.

The Gospel calls Joseph "a just man." What does this mean? It means "a perfect man, one who has all virtues.". . . St. Joseph talked with Christ for thirty years. Joseph listened to His lifegiving words. He saw the perfect example of humbleness and patience that He gave, the promptness with which He obeyed and helped His foster-father in his work, and in all the household tasks. Jesus' burning charity must have kindled a great fire of Divine Love in Joseph's heart — a heart that was altogether free from earthly affections. . . . Joseph's love for his wife filled him still more with Divine Love. Accordingly, we cannot doubt that, during the time he spent with Jesus, he was raised to such a height of holiness and merit as to surpass those of all other saints.

By Our Lord's grace, there is today not a Catholic in the world who is not devout toward St. Joseph; and, among them all, those who recommend themselves to him most often and with the most trust and confidence receive graces most abundantly. Never let a day pass, then, without recommending ourselves to St. Joseph. . . . I urge you to ask for three special graces in particular: forgiveness of your sins, love for Jesus Christ and a good death. Could a sinner who sought forgiveness from Our Lord have found a more effective means of obtaining it than through St. Joseph?. . .

If the two disciples who were going to Emmaus were inflamed with divine love by the few moments they spent in the company of our Savior and by His words inspiring them to say 'were not our hearts burning within us, while He spoke on the way?' What flames of holy love must have been enkindled in the heart of St. Joseph, who for thirty years conversed with Jesus Christ and listened to his words of eternal life.

Fr. Alban Butler

Fr. Alban Butler (1710–1773) most famous for his publication *Lives of the Saints* in which he spent 30 years compiling information on over 1600 saints. He wrote that St. Joseph's true glory consisted in his humility and virtue. The history of his life has not been written by men; but his principal actions are recorded by the Holy Spirit himself. God entrusted him with the education of His Divine Son.... He sent an angel from Heaven, not to reprehend anything in Joseph's holy conduct but to dissipate all his doubts and fears, by revealing to him this adorable mystery....

Pope Clement XI approved a Proper Mass and Office on February 4, 1714 for the feast of St. Joseph. Pope Benedict XIII, on December 19, 1726, inserted the name of St. Joseph in the Litany of the Saints.

China

In China, missionaries obtained permission from the Emperor to carry on their activities and preach the Gospel. They erected a votive chapel in honor of St. Joseph at Peking in addition to the three churches they built previously. In the year 1730 there was an earthquake which took about 500,000 lives but the votive chapel remained unharmed. The missionaries also were left unharmed.

Philadelphia

In 1733 Old Saint Joseph's Church was founded. This was the first church in Philadelphia and one of the first Catholic Churches in the original colonies. Old St. Joseph's was founded by Jesuits, specifically Fr. Joseph Greaton and Fr. Joseph Felix Barbelin. Fr. Greaton was born in 1678 in Devonshire, England.

Fr. Greaton came to Philadelphia permanently in 1729. He had been a convert to Catholicism and was ordained a priest in 1704. Fr. Greaton began the erection of a Jesuit mansion in 1731 and Mass was first said in the residence at 4th Street near Willings Alley on February 26, 1732.

By 1735 the Patronage of St. Joseph was generally observed throughout Spain on the third Sunday after Easter.

Pope Benedict XIV (Pope 1740–58) shows that St. Joseph's name was inscribed in the Roman Martyrology before the Eighth Century (The nineteenth day of March, in Judea, the birthday of St. Joseph, spouse of Blessed Mary the Virgin, Confessor). He also notes that St. Joseph's name was invoked publicly in the Litanies of Bologna.

Frances Allen

A remarkable conversion took place through the intercession of St. Joseph. Frances Allen, a young American Protestant, the daughter of Ethan Allen the American patriot and soldier of the Revolutionary War. Her mother, Francoise Montresor lost her heroic husband when Frances was very young and later married Dr. Jabez Penniman. While not an atheist, he was sufficiently adverse to religion to exclude every thought of it, as far as possible, from his stepdaughter's mind.

Endowed with a precocious and penetrating mind, Miss Allen applied herself to reading. Having access to only romances and works by Deists, she became an unbeliever, even before knowing religious truths.

As it happened when she was twelve years old, while she was walking on the edge of a river and gazing at the turbulent water, she saw a huge monster swimming towards her which caused her great fear. What increased her terror was the fact that she seemed unable to turn her eyes away from the monster, and it was impossible for her to make the slightest movement in order to escape.

In this painful dilemma she seemed to perceive an old man near her, bald and covered with a brown mantle, a staff in his hand, who taking her by the arm, said: "Little girl what are you doing there? Flee!" She did so quickly.

When she was at some distance she looked back to see the old man, but he had disappeared. As soon as she reached home, her mother, seeing her troubled look and her face so pale, understood that something extraordinary had happened to her.

The child related the cause of her fright and the assistance given her by an unknown man. The mother sent, at once, a servant to find him in order to thank him for his kindness; but the search was in vain — they never knew what became of the old man.

Eleven years later, Miss Allen, not being a Catholic, and having heard people speak of Catholics unfavorably, wished to ascertain whether what was said of them was true. In order to learn more of Catholicism, she asked her parents permission to go to Montreal under the pretense to learn French. Before her departure, her parents required her to be baptized by the Reverend Daniel Barber, a Presbyterian Minister of Claremont, New Hampshire. She resisted but finally complied with their wishes. Being an unbeliever, she laughed during the ceremony, for which Rev. Barber reprimanded her severely.

She attended boarding school conducted by the Sisters of the Congregation of Our Lady, in order to study French. One day a Sister asked her to place on the altar a vase of flowers which she had prepared, and at the same time requested her to adore our Lord in entering the chapel. The young girl went away laughing, resolved not to genuflect before the altar. Arriving at the entrance to the chapel she attempts to enter the sanctuary. But suddenly feels she can go no further — she makes several attempts to advance, but in vain.

Finally, feeling the real presence of our Lord, she falls on her knees and adores Jesus Christ. She immediately withdraws to the entrance of the chapel, all in tears, and resolves to give herself to the service of God. She did not mention to her teachers what had occurred, but requested to be instructed in the Catholic Faith. Shortly afterwards she consented to go to confession. After completing her course of instruction she made her solemn abjuration and was baptized by Father Le Saulnier, Vicar of Montreal, her former baptism being made invalid by reason of the lack of consent on her part. When she made her First Communion, she felt within her an unmistakable vocation to the religious life.

When her parents were informed of her conversion, they came to Montreal and took her home. They attempted to obliterate the idea of becoming a religious by bestowing on her every worldly pleasure and social enjoyment, but as soon as the year ended, which she had consented to spend with them before making any further decisions, she declared to her parents her final decision. Her mother desiring her daughter's happiness, finally consented and accompanied her to Montreal.

Now a Catholic, she wished to embrace the religious life; and in order to know her vocation she visited the churches of Montreal, among others that of the Hôtel-Dieu, under the direction of the Sisters of St. Joseph.

No sooner had she cast her eyes on the painting of the main-altar, which represents the Holy Family, and fixed her gaze on the face of St. Joseph than she cried out to her mother who accompanied her: "This is his picture you see, mother, St. Joseph wants me here — it is he who saved my life by shielding me from the monster that wished to devour me."

It was indeed, the face and the costume of the venerable old man whom she had seen thirteen years before.

She had no doubt that St. Joseph wished to save her from the monster to heresy and unbelief by leading her to the convent dedicated to his honor and to salvation.

She entered the novitiate of the Daughters of St. Joseph and made her religious profession in 1808. She became a model of all Christian virtues and an instrument in God's hands for the conversion of a large number of non-catholics.

The attack on the authority of the Papacy is finally brought to an end with the French Revolution (1789–1799) which closes out the Eighteenth Century.

CHAPTER SEVEN

With the advent of the Nineteenth Century an exciting stage of history begins. The cult of St. Joseph starts to take on a new aspect as the Papacy becomes more vocal. The Church starts to give even more recognition to St. Joseph.

St. Madeleine Sophie Barat

St. Madeleine Sophie Barat (Dec 12, 1779–May 25, 1865) spoke the following: "The two greatest personages who ever lived on this earth subjected themselves to St. Joseph. Jesus wished to become indebted to him for the necessities of life, and of the Holy Patriarch alone it may be said that He saved the life of this Savior. Let us love Jesus above all. Let us love Mary as our Mother, but then, how could we keep from loving Joseph, who was so intimately united to both Jesus and Mary? And how can we honor him better than by imitating his virtues? Now, what else did he do in all his life but contemplate, study and adore Jesus, even in the midst of his daily labors? Behold, therefore, our model."

Jacques Dujarie

Father Jacques Dujarie founded the Congregation of the Brothers of St. Joseph in 1820 at Ruille-sur-Loir, in Le Mans diocese, France.

The background for the contemporary apostle of St. Joseph begins. On September 27, 1831 Isaac Bessette and Clothilde Foisy are married. They are to be the parents of Alfred Bessette, later to be known as Brother André, for whom history will record as perhaps the most outstanding apostle of St. Joseph. This will be disclosed later in our story.

Basil Moreau

Fr. Basil Moreau founded the order of the Auxiliary Priests of Le Mans 1833, located in LeMans, France. Fr. Moreau's dream was to establish an International Shrine to St. Joseph.

In 1835 Fr. Moreau succeeded Fr. Dujarie as superior of the Brothers of St. Joseph, and transfers them to LeMans, France. On March 1, 1837, Fr. Moreau unites the priests of Le Mans with the Brothers of St. Joseph which marks the official foundation of the Congregation of Holy Cross.

St. Pierre Julien Eymard

St. Pierre Julien Eymard (1811–68) was ordained in 1834. He was the founder of the Congregation of the Blessed Sacrament. He speaks of the revelation given him by our Lord. "Our Lord has given me today a singular grace. He has inspired me to dedicate myself in a special manner to St. Joseph as my father, leader and protector. . . . He will be the spiritual director of my interior life, in order that I may lead that same life with him, hidden with Jesus and Mary and with his own self. I will imitate him especially in his silence regarding himself…"

"I dedicated myself to St. Joseph in all my duties as superior, so that I may fulfill these duties as I should, being meek and humble of heart as he himself was, endeavoring to be meek of heart with my brethren, humble with myself, and simple before God. I have chosen this good saint to be my counselor and bosom friend. I have taken him for my protector in troubles and difficulties, and for the protector of my congregation, being the little family of Jesus. I have not asked him to free me from my crosses and trials, but only from that self-love which spoils them and turns them into arguments of vanity."

"I have prayed to our Lord that He might give me St. Joseph for a father, as he had given me Mary for a Mother; that He might put in my heart that devotion, that confidence, that filial love of a client, of a devotee of St. Joseph. I trust the good Master has heard my prayers, for I now feel greater devotion to this great saint, and I am full of confidence and hope."

In an introduction on St. Joseph, the following explanation is given to Fr. Eymard's love of St. Joseph. The special vocation and mission which each saint receives from God marks with a particular stamp his spiritual doctrine. Even his devotion to the saints is strongly influenced by this predominant vocational grace. He will, for instance, have a greater devotion to certain saints whose vocation and spiritual characteristics bear close resemblance to his own.

St. Peter Julian Eymard, we know, had one all absorbing devotion, the Blessed Sacrament. Ever since the day when, as a small child, he had heard his pious mother whisper to him as she pointed to the tabernacle, "Jesus is there," his whole life had been centered in the Blessed Sacrament. This thought of the God-Man dwelling in the Eucharist through love of man gradually took complete possession of him to the extent of obsessing him—we may even say distracting him continually. Indeed we may safely affirm that no saint, ancient or modern, was ever granted in a fuller measure, the eucharistic grace, or ever corresponded to it more faithfully.

It is not surprising, therefore, to note that St. Peter Julian Eymard's devotion to the foster-father of Jesus was strongly tinged with a eucharistic character. First and foremost, he considered St. Joseph as the perfect adorer of our Lord on earth. Where other saints saw in St. Joseph the Father of the Poor, the Ideal Husband, the Model Working man, the Patron of a

Good Death. St. Peter Julian saw the accomplished Model Adorer. He considered in St. Joseph his complete self-surrender and entire devotedness in the service of the Word Incarnate. In this he found St. Joseph an inspiring model of the service and adoration of the Blessed Sacrament which he was to preach throughout the length and breadth of France. He would have his spiritual sons carry their imitation of St. Joseph even to the point of identifying themselves with him in their service of adoration of the Blessed Sacrament: "let us be the Josephs of the Eucharist as he was the Joseph of Nazareth."

Bishop Ignace Bourget

Bishop Ignace Bourget (Oct. 30, 1799 to June 8, 1885) was born in the province of Quebec. At the age of 22 he was named secretary to Bishop Lartigue, the first bishop of Montreal. Bishop Plessis observed at that time: "If Bishop Lartigue is not content with his new secretary, I can do no more, for he has the best." On November 30, 1822, he was ordained a priest by Bishop Lartigue. At the age of 23, he was already a priest and secretary to the Bishop! On April 19, 1840 he became the second bishop of Montreal and was the builder of the diocese of Montreal, encompassing areas from Montreal to Ottawa.

Bishop Bourget went to France in 1841 to ask Fr. Moreau for missionaries for Canada. These two men formed a strange bargain: Bishop Bourget purchased nine religious by giving Fr. Moreau the relic of a four year old martyr who had been put to death during the early persecutions. This was possible since Bishop Bourget had brought the body from Rome.

Bishop Bourget had a dream, "We must have a church specifically dedicated to St. Joseph's cult in which St. Joseph may receive daily the public homage worthy of his eminent virtues. . . . We wish to consecrate all our strength and the rest of our life to making him honored in such a church, establishing a place of pilgrimage where the people will come to him."

In 1841, the first Holy Cross religious arrive from France, at an Indian settlement in South Bend, Indiana (located in St. Joseph County on the south bend of the St. Joseph River) to establish what is known today as the University of Notre Dame.

Little Sisters of the Poor

Jeanne Jugan (1792–1889) founded the Little Sisters of the Poor in 1839 at St. Servan, France. She had great devotion to St. Joseph and designated him as patron and protector of all their homes in which God's aged poor are tenderly guarded and served. There are numerous stories of St. Joseph's intercession on behalf of the sisters and their charges. The general procedure was to place their petition at the base of St. Joseph's statue. If possible they would place a picture of the item desired.

One example occurred at the Home of the Holy Trinity in Angers, France. There was no more butter to spread on the old women's crusts, or that of the Little Sisters. In the evening on her return from collecting, Jeanne was greeted by the Sister in charge of the Refectory, who was upset by their predicament. "What!" Jeanne cried, "there's no more butter, and you haven't asked St. Joseph for any?" Then she went into the little room which was used as a parlor, arranged the empty butter dishes in the center of the table, placed one of them upside down and with due respect, placed on this improvised pedestal a statuette of the Holy Patriarch. But would their visitors understand? "Write," said Jeanne, presenting her with a wide strip of paper, "write in large capitals: 'Kind St.

Joseph, send us some butter for our poor old women.'"

The inscription was placed before the statuette and a votive light was left burning at its feet. The Sisters waited to see what the effects of their "childish confidence" would bring. One of the Sisters recorded that "a few days later, a large quantity of butter was brought to the Home; no one ever knew by whom."

Numerous other instances have been expounded by the Sisters where St. Joseph has interceded to provide food, a typewriter and any other need that may be required to give service to their charges. However, they give a warning. The experience of the Sisters has been that whatever favor may be desired is granted according to the way it is asked. For instance, potatoes were needed. The Sisters had only a sprouting potato. This was placed at the feet of St. Joseph's statue, with the request that he obtain potatoes. In a day or two a farmer brought a number of sacks of potatoes "sprouting."

Another example was at one of their Brooklyn Homes. The old men had no beer to drink for some time, so the old men placed their empty cans in front of St. Joseph's statue to remind him of their need. A Priest visiting the Home passed the statue and asked the Good Mother what the beer cans were doing in front of the statue. She told him that the old men were asking St. Joseph for beer. On his way back to his rectory on the subway the Priest was enjoying a private chuckle over the story, when a stranger who sat opposite came over and asked to share the joke. The priest told him the story, and the stranger announced that as vice-president of a large beer company he would see that the old men would never want for beer again as long as he lived. Within a few days a large delivery of beer was made to the Home of the Little Sisters of the Poor with the stranger's compliments.

The last example shows the poignancy of asking for exactly what you desire. In one of their Homes they were in need of a man to help in the kitchen. They clipped from a newspaper the picture of a nice old man, and placed it at the feet of St. Joseph. They had not noticed that in cutting out the picture they had cut off one arm. A few days later a destitute old man, with but one arm, came and asked to be taken into the Home, stating that he would like to help the sisters with their work. He was assigned to the kitchen and rendered many services.

The Little Sisters of the Poor rely on St. Joseph for all their needs even today. They give us a great example to follow in having confidence in St. Joseph.

William Frederick Faber

William Frederick Faber (1814–63) was a priest of the Congregation of the Oratory in London. He wrote much about St. Joseph, specifically during the late 1840's and 1850's. He says that God's time had come for "this dear devotion" to St. Joseph.

The following are excepts from Fr. Faber's book *Bethlehem.* St. Joseph presents us with a similar, yet somewhat different, type of devotion to the Sacred Infancy (to that of the Blessed Virgin). We know nothing of the beginnings of this wonderful saint. . . . He was doubtless high in sanctity before his espousal with Mary. God's eternal choice of him would seem to imply as much. During the nine months the accumulation of grace upon him must have been beyond our powers of calculation. The company of Mary, the atmosphere of Jesus, the continual presence of the Incarnate God, and the fact of his own life being nothing but a series of ministries to the unborn Word, must have lifted him far above all other saints, and perchance all angels too. Our Lord's birth, and the sight of His face, must have been to him like another sanctification. The mystery of Bethlehem was enough of itself to place him among the highest of the saints. As with Mary, self-abasement was his grandest grace. He was conscious to himself that he was the shadow of the Eternal Father, and this knowledge overwhelmed him.... Commanding makes deep men more humble than obeying. St. Joseph's humility was fed all through life by having to command Jesus, by being the superior of his God. The priest, who has most reason to deplore the lack of his attainments in humility, is humble at least when he comes to consecrate at Mass. For years, Joseph lived in awe of that, which to the priest is but a moment. The little house at Nazareth was as the outspread square of the white corporal. All the words he spoke were almost words of consecration.

To be hidden in God, to be lost in his bright light, is surely the highest of vocations among the sons of men. Nothing, to a spiritually discerning eye, can surpass the grandeur of a life which is only for others, only ministering to the divine purposes as in the place of God, without any personal vocation or any purpose of its own. He lives now only to serve the Infant Jesus, as heretofore he has but lived to guard Mary, the lily of God. He is the head of the Holy Family, only that, like a good superior, he may more completely be the servant and the subject and the instrument.... He passes noiselessly into the shadow of eternity, like the moon behind a cloud, complaining not that her silver light is intercepted.... His spirit is the spirit of Bethlehem. He is, in a special way, the property of the Sacred Infancy. He was raised to the further and inexpressible dignity of likeness to the Son Himself, who was also the image of the Father....

In Fr. Faber's book *The Blessed Sacrament,* he further expounds on St. Joseph, the foster-father and his child.

St. Joseph is in Bethlehem, Egypt, the Wilderness and Nazareth, as the shadow of the Eternal Father. This is the immensity of his dignity. To the world without, he passes for Jesus's Father. The unspeakable treasures of God, Jesus and Mary, are committed to St. Joseph's keeping; and he is himself a treasure, as well as the treasure-house of God. He is part of the scheme of Redemption. . . .

The adoration of Jesus and the devotion to Mary had taken their places immovably in the sense of the faithful and in the practical system of the Church, one shedding light upon the other, and both instructing, illuminating, nourishing and sanctifying the people. . . . But there was still one more of the "earthly trinity," as it is called. Devotion to St. Joseph lay dormant in the Church. Tradition held some scanty notices of him; but they had no light but what they borrowed from St. Matthew. All we have now of St. Joseph was there then; only the sense of the faithful had not taken it up; God's time was not yet come. The sense of the faithful was not like the complete science of the Apostles. It was not equal to it. It had to grow to it, to master it, to fill it out with devotions, to animate it with institutions, to submit to it as a perfectly administered hierarchy. But God's time came for this dear devotion; and it came like all His gifts when times were dark and calamities were rife.

An electric current seemed to circulate through the hearts of the faithful and not only through Europe, but wherever Christians were to be found. He continues in his work on the Blessed Sacrament with a concise summary of devotion to St. Joseph. "Gerson was raised up to be its doctor and theologian, St. Teresa to be its saint, and St. Francis de Sales to be its popular leader and missioner. The houses of Carmel were like the Holy House of Nazareth to it, and the colleges of the Jesuits its peaceful sojourns in dark Egypt. The contemplative took it up, and fed upon it; the active laid hold of it, and nursed the sick and fed the hungry in its name. The working people fastened on it, for both the saint and his devotion were of them. The young were drawn to it and it made them pure, the aged rested on it, for it made them peaceful." St. Sulpice took it, and it became the spirit of the Secular Clergy. And when the great Society of Jesus had taken refuge in the Sacred Heart, and the Fathers of the Sacred Heart were keeping their lamps burning ready for the resurrection of the Society, devotion to St. Joseph was their stay and their consolation, and they cast the seeds of a new devotion, to the Heart of Joseph, which will some day flourish and abound. So it gathered into itself orders and congregations, high and low, young and old, ecclesiastical and lay, schools and confraternities, hospitals, orphanages and penitentiaries, everywhere holding up Jesus, everywhere hand in hand with Mary, everywhere the refreshing shadow of the Eternal Father. Then when it had filled Europe with its odor, it went over the Atlantic, plunged into the damp umbrage of the back woods, embraced all Canada, became a mighty missionary power, and tens of thousands of savages filled the forests and the rolling prairies at sundown with hymns to St. Joseph, the praises of the foster-father of our Lord. (The Bishop of Buffalo, New York, Msgr. Timon, told Fr. Faber that when he laid the foundation-stone of his new cathedral in Buffalo, all his school children were gathered round him, and at his bidding sang the Oratory hymn to St. Joseph.)

Of the small number of devotions to St. Joseph which have been indulgenced by the Holy See, two are for priests only. The one to be said before Mass, speaks "not only of seeing and bearing Jesus, but of carrying Him, kissing Him, clothing Him and taking care of Him," and then says "O God, who has given unto us a royal priesthood, grant that as Blessed Joseph deserved reverently to touch with his hands and carry Your Only-begotten Son born of the Virgin Mary, we too may serve at Your altars;" and again in the collect called "The Efficacious Prayer," also indulgenced by Pius VII, for priests only, St. Joseph is spoken of as the keeper of the Virgins, Jesus and Mary, and the models of our ministration to Them both. But look at the parallel between St. Joseph and the Catholic priesthood. Was he the steward of God's House? So are they. Was he the dispenser of God's gifts, as the Church calls him? So are they. Was he the keeper of the Bread of life? So are they. Did he handle, carry, lift up and lay down the Body of Jesus? So do they. If Jesus was subject to him, so is He, and even more wonderfully, to them.

In Fr. Faber's book, *The Foot of the Cross,* he speaks of the sorrows of Mary and Joseph. The first sorrow comes through Simeon while at the Temple. In the second sorrow, with the threat of Jesus life, it is Joseph who is told to flee to Egypt. There is a certain appearance of cruelty in sending sorrow through those we love. As they must flee into Egypt, it was at once a sorrow to Joseph to convey fresh sadness to Mary, and for Her to receive it from him.

Brother André

August 9, 1845 is an auspicious day in the cultus of St. Joseph. Alfred Bessette was born at St. Gregoire d'Iberville, Canada. The importance of this man in the propagation of devotion to St. Joseph requires a more in depth study which will be covered in a later chapter.

Holy Cross

In 1847, the religious are sent by Fr. Moreau to Saint Laurent, near Montreal in Canada. Bishop Bourget actually received two priests, eight brothers and four sisters in keeping with Fr. Moreau's concept of his order as a family with priests, brothers and sisters functioning as a unit.

Pius IX extends the feast of the Patronage of St. Joseph to the whole Church as a Double rite of the Second Class on September 10, 1847.

John Henry Cardinal Newman

John Henry Cardinal Newman (1801–90) was an English Cardinal, Theologian and author, beginning as a leader in the Oxford Movement. The Oxford Movement, in the Church of England, was based on Tractarianism. It sought to link the Anglican Church more closely to the Roman Catholic Church and opposed liberalism in theology. A Tractarian was one of the authors of *Tracts for the Times* (1833–41), a series of 90 religious pamphlets written by and expressing the views of members of the Oxford Movement, also a supporter or adherent of this group.

In 1826 Cardinal Newman became Vicar of St. Mary's, the Anglican Church at the University of Oxford. He thus became a leader of the Oxford Group and chief contributor to *Tracts for the Times*. The final Tract provoked a storm of opposition by its claim that the 39 articles of the Church of England which incorporate the creed of the Reformed Church in England are aimed primarily at the abuses and not the dogmas of Roman Catholicism. In 1842 he retired from Oxford and October 9, 1845 resigned his post as Vicar for St. Mary's and then became a Roman Catholic. In 1846 Cardinal Newman went to Rome and was ordained a priest and entered the Congregation of the Oratory. He spent most of his life at the House of the Oratory which he established near Birmingham, England. During the period of 1854–58, he served as Rector of a Catholic University that the Bishops of Ireland were attempting to establish in Dublin. Pope Leo XIII elevated him to Cardinal in 1879.

With this background, it is interesting that Cardinal Newman should write on the devotion to the saints from the perspective of the convert, especially devotion to St. Joseph. The following are excerpts from his writings.

By "faith" I mean the Creed and assent to the Creed; by "devotion" I mean such religious honors as belong to the objects of our faith, and the payment of those honors. Faith and devotion are as distinct in fact as they are in idea. We cannot, indeed, be devout without faith, but we may believe without feeling devotion.... For instance, a great author, or a public man, may be acknowledged as such for a course of years; yet there may be an increase, an ebb and flow in his popularity. And if he takes a lasting place in the minds of his countrymen, he may gradually grow into it, or suddenly be raised to it.... Illustrations, though not altogether opposite, serve to convey that distinction between faith and devotion on which I am insisting....

This distinction is forcibly brought home to a convert, as a peculiarity of the Catholic religion, on his first introduction to its worship. The faith is everywhere one and the same, but a large liberty is accorded to private judgement and inclination as regards matters of devotion. Any large church, with its collections and groups of people, will illustrate this. The fabric itself is dedicated to Almighty God, and that, under the invocation of the Blessed Virgin, or some particular saint; or again, of some mystery belonging to the Divine Name or the Incarnation, or some mystery associated with the Blessed Virgin. Perhaps there are seven altars or more in it, and these again have their several saints. Then there is the feast proper to this or that day; and during the celebration of Mass, of all the worshipers who crowd around the priest, each has his own particular devotions, with which he follows the rite. . . . Then there are confraternities attached to the church of the Sacred Heart, or of the Precious Blood; associations of prayer for a good death, or for the repose of departed souls, or for the conversion of the heathen; devotions connected with the brown, blue or red scapular; not to speak of the great ordinary ritual observed through the four seasons, or the constant Presence of the Blessed Sacrament, or of its ever-recurring rite of Benediction, and its extraordinary forty hours expostion.

The first of these sacred observances, long before such national memories, were the devotions paid to the Apostles, then those which were paid to the martyrs; yet there were saints nearer to our Lord than either martyrs or Apostles; but, as if these sacred persons were immersed and lost in the effulgence of His glory, and because they did not manifest themselves, when in the body, in external works separate from Him, it happened that for a long while they were less dwelt upon. . . . New creations of God's power, took their place, or again, the saints of some religious order here or there established. . . . Those names, I say, which at first sight might have been expected to enter soon into the devotions of the faithful, with better reason might have been looked for at a later date, and actually were late in their coming.

St. Joseph furnishes the most striking instance of this remark; here is the clearest instance of the distinction between doctrine and devotion. Who, from his prerogatives and the testimony on which they come to us, had a greater claim to receive an early recognition among the faithful than he? A saint of Scripture, the foster father of Our Lord, he was an object of the universal and absolute faith of the Christian world from the first, yet the devotion to him is comparatively of late date. When once it began, men seemed surprised that it had not been thought of before; and now they hold him next to the Blessed Virgin in their religious affection and veneration.

In 1854, Pope Pius IX issued the solemn decree declaring the Immaculate Conception to be dogma for the belief of the Universal Church. In 1858 Bernadette Soubirous of Lourdes was chosen to spread the cultus of the Immaculate Conception, shortly after the official proclamation of that dogma. We will later find a similar comparison between Brother André and St. Joseph.

In 1855, Bishop Bourget reaffirms his dream, through a letter to all the churches in Montreal. He wishes to have a Universal Church dedicated to St. Joseph, in order that the people can show their honor to St. Joseph.

Herbert Cardinal Vaughan

Herbert Cardinal Vaughan (1831–1903), the third archbishop of Westminster, England in 1866 founded St. Joseph College, at Mill Hill near London. He was also the founder of the Missionaries of St. Joseph. In 1883 he founded the Franciscan Missionary Sisters of St. Joseph.

Cardinal Vaughan wrote an article entitled *Go to Joseph*.

Who is St. Joseph?

Joseph, the son of the patriarch Jacob, was the figure of St. Joseph, the son of another Jacob; "Jacob begot Joseph, the husband of Mary, of whom was born Jesus, who is called the Christ" (Matt 1:16).

What was truly said of the first Joseph, as to his future, and as to his goodness, his chastity, his patience, his wisdom, his influence with the king, his power over the people and his love for his brethren, is verified much more perfectly, even to this day, in the second Joseph.

Of old it was said to the needy and suffering people in the kingdom of Egypt: "Go to Joseph, and do all that he shall say to you" (Gen. 41:55). The same is now said by the Sovereign Pontiff to all needy and suffering people in the Kingdom of the Church — "Go to Joseph."

If you labor for your bread; if you have a family to support; if your heart is searched by trials at home; if you are assailed by some persistent temptation; if your faith is sorely tested, and your hope seems lost in darkness and disappointment; if you have yet to learn to love and serve Jesus and Mary, the nursing father of Jesus—Joseph is your model, your teacher and your father. Truly, in all things, St. Joseph is the people's friend.

Go, then to Joseph, and do all that he shall say to you.

Go to Joseph, and obey him as Jesus and Mary obeyed him.

Go to Joseph, and speak to him as they spoke to him.

Go to Joseph, and consult him as they consulted him.

Go to Joseph, and honor him as they honored him.

Go to Joseph, and be grateful to him as they were grateful to him.

Go to Joseph, and love him as they loved him, and as they love him still.

However much you love Joseph, your love will always fall short of the extraordinary love which Jesus and Mary bore to him. On the other hand, the love of Joseph necessarily leads us to Jesus and Mary. He was the first Christian to whom it was said, "Take the Child and His mother. . . . " This led a Father of the Church to say, "You will always find Jesus with Mary and Joseph."

"Joseph and Marie" by Petrus von Schendel (1858)

St. Bernadette Soubirous

St. Bernadette Soubirous (1844–1879) who took the name Sr. Marie-Bernard upon entering convent life. In 1867 at the height of her religious career and enjoying fairly good health, assisted with the care of patients in the infirmary. An example of her normal day at that time is as follows:

She would arrive at the infirmary at about 8:00 in the morning, visit with the patients then leave and return with their breakfast trays. At noontime, she used to recite the Angelus, serve the meals and wash the dishes. Only after this midday chore did she find a few minutes to relax in the garden. It was then that she would state that she would visit her father.

One day one of the sisters, hearing this, asked the Reverend Mother "Aren't Bernadette's parents still living in Lourdes?" "Indeed they are," came the reply, "but it was St. Joseph whom Sr. Marie-Bernard meant and the chapel in the garden was the place where she kept her rendezvous with him."

Interestingly enough, Bernadette rests within the walls of the chapel, dedicated to St. Joseph, in the garden of her cloister.

As we close out the first 70 years of the Nineteenth Century, we find an atmosphere within the Papacy ready to give the recognition to St. Joseph that has been proclaimed in varying degrees for more than 1800 years. We should note that there is no saint, other than the Blessed Mother, whom the church honors more than St. Joseph, dedicating every Wednesday and the entire month of March to him.

CHAPTER EIGHT

Pope Pius IX

The Nineteenth Century continues with the preliminaries to the official declaration of St. Joseph as Patron of the Universal Church. On March 9, 1870 a petition was presented to the Vatican Council by 43 Generals of Religious Orders, asking that St. Joseph be declared Patron of the Universal Church. Also two other petitions signed by 255 and 118 Bishops respectively were presented. These petitions are printed in *Collectio acensis.*

St. Joseph is made Patron of the Universal Church on December 8, 1870 by Pope Pius IX, who also reinforced March as the Month of St. Joseph and approved his confraternity. The full decree was called *Quemadmodum Deus* and we print the complete translation because of it's importance.

"As Almighty God appointed Joseph, son the patriarch Jacob, over all the land of Egypt to save grain for the people, so when the fullness of time was come and he was about to send on earth his Only-begotten Son, the Savior of the World, he chose another Joseph, whom He made lord and chief of His household and possessions, the guardian of His choicest Treasures.

So also (Joseph) had as his spouse the Immaculate Virgin Mary, and of Her was born by the Holy Spirit, Jesus Christ our Lord, Who in the sight of men deigned to be reputed the son of Joseph, and was subject to him.

And so it was that Him Whom countless kings and prophets had of old desired to see, Joseph not only saw but conversed with, and embraced in paternal affection, and kissed, and most diligently reared even Him whom the faithful were to receive as the Bread that came down from Heaven that they might obtain eternal life.

Because of this sublime dignity which God conferred on His most faithful servant, the Church has always most highly honored and praised Blessed Joseph next to his spouse, the Virgin Mother of God, and has besought his intercession in times of trouble.

And now therefore, when in these most troublesome times the Church is beset by enemies on every side and is weighed down by calamities so heavy that ungodly men assert that the gates of hell have at length prevailed against Her, the venerable prelates of the Catholic world have presented to the Sovereign Pontiff their own petitions and those of the faithful committed to their charge, praying that he would deign to constitute St. Joseph, Patron of the Universal Church. And this time their prayer and desire was renewed by them even more earnestly at the Sacred Ecumenical Council of the Vatican.

Accordingly, it has now pleased our Most Holy Sovereign Pius IX, Pope, deeply affected by the recent deplorable events, to comply with the desires of the prelates and to commit to St. Joseph's most powerful patronage, himself, and all the faithful. He therefore has declared St. Joseph, Patron of the Universal Church."

We should note that this was more of an official proclamation for recognition of St. Joseph's patronage over the Church. This decree mentions the great power of St. Joseph's intercession, which needs to be reinforced in our own time.

Pope Pius IX said, "I have seen a little picture which represents Joseph with the Divine Infant, Who points towards him, saying: 'Ite ad Joseph!' To you I say the same. Go to Joseph! Have recourse with special confidence to St. Joseph, for his protection is most powerful, as he is the Patron of the Universal Church."

Inclytum Patriarcham

Pope Pius IX summarizes the past history of the Feast of St. Joseph in *Inclytum Patriarcham* on July 7, 1871. It lays down rules for its worthy celebration in the Liturgy. The complete text follows:

"The Catholic Church rightly honors with its highest cultus and venerates with a feeling of deep reverence the illustrious Patriarch, Blessed Joseph, now crowned with glory and honor in Heaven, whom Almighty God, in preference to all his saints, willed on earth to be the chaste and true spouse of the Immaculate Virgin Mary as well as the putative father of His Only-begotten Son. He indeed enriched him and filled him to overflowing with entirely unique graces, enabling him to execute most faithfully the duties of so sublime a state.

Wherefore, the Roman Pontiffs, Our Predecessors, in order that they might daily increase and more ardently stimulate in the hearts of the Christian faithful a reverence and devotion for the Holy Patriarch, and that further they might exhort them to implore with utmost confidence his intercession with God, have not failed to decree for him new and ever greater tokens of public veneration whenever the occasion served.

Among these let it suffice to call to mind Our Predecessors of happy memory, Sixtus IV, who wished the feast of St. Joseph to be inserted in the Roman Missal and Breviary; Gregory XV, who by a decree of May 8, 1621, ordered that the Feast should be observed in the whole world, under a double precept; Clement X, who on December 6, 1670 afforded to the Feast the rite of a double of the second class; Clement XI, who by a decree of February 4, 1714, adorned the Feast with a complete proper Mass and office; and finally Benedict XIII, who by a decree published on December 19, 1726, ordered the name of the Holy Patriarch to be added to the Litany of the Saints.

We ourselves, raised to the Supreme Chair of Peter by the inscrutable design of God, and moved by the example of our illustrious predecessors, as well as by the singular devotion which from youth itself we entertained toward the Holy Patriarch, have by a decree of September 10, 1847, extended with great joy of soul the Feast of His Patronage to the Whole Church, under the rite of double of the second class — a Feast which was already being celebrated in many places by a special indult of the Holy See.

However, in these latter times in which a monstrous and most abominable war has been declared against the Church of Christ, the devotion of the faithful toward St. Joseph has grown and progressed to such an extent that from every direction innumerable and fervent petitions have once more reached us. These were recently renewed during the Second Ecumenical Council of the Vatican by groups of the faithful, and — what is more important — by many of our Venerable Brethren, the Cardinals and Bishops of the Holy Roman Church.

In their petitions, they begged of us that in these mournful days, as a safeguard against the evils which disturb us on every side, we should more efficaciously implore the compassion of God through the merits and intercession of St. Joseph, declaring him Patron of the Universal Church. Accordingly, moved by these requests and after having invoked the Divine Light, we deemed it right that desires in such numbers and of such piety should be granted. . . ."

The author would like to draw attention to the first paragraph. Nowhere else, even in the monumental encyclical of Leo XIII (1889), can there be found in church documents a paragraph which better summarizes the position of St. Joseph. These sentences must be ranked among the choicest ever uttered about the saint. They teach that (1) Joseph is granted extreme high honors among the saints; (2) God predestined him for a unique vocation in preference to all other saints; (3) He was the genuine, virginal husband of Mary; (4) He fulfilled a fatherly position with respect to Jesus, being thought publicly to be Christ's natural father and acting with a father's rights; (5) His position is entirely unique; and (6) He carried out his duties with perfect fidelity to God's grace.

The Miracle Staircase

True stories regarding the intercession of St. Joseph abound. One that has become known to the general public is "the miracle staircase". In 1872 the bishop of Santa Fe, New Mexico commissioned the building of a convent chapel, Our Lady of Light Chapel in the care of the Sisters of Loretto. During the course of its construction the architect died suddenly and only afterwards did the builders discover an error in the plans. There was no staircase to the choir loft. But worse, at that point of construction, any stairwell would take up needed space and disfigure the design.

The nuns began nine days of prayer in honor of St. Joseph, for he was a carpenter. On the day after their novena ended, a shabbily dressed man appeared at the door. The Sisters showed him their choir loft and the limited space available to erect a staircase. He assured them he would be able to build one, and so they let him undertake the task. With him was a burro carrying his tool box. He offered to begin at once, if they would allow him total privacy while he worked. They hired him and he locked himself in. For three months he permitted no visitors; then he opened the doors.

The staircase in Our Lady of Light Chapel, Santa Fe, New Mexico

When the Mother Superior entered, she stared in amazement. there in the corner was a beautiful free standing staircase rising in a double spiral to the choir loft that may be seen today by visitors to Santa Fe. Each section is perfectly fitted in a groove, — not a nail being used in its construction. There is no central pole, no wall attachment, no sign of a nail or screw — just a few wooden pegs. Moreover, the wood he used was unlike any the Mother had ever seen. Yet the carpenter had brought no wood with him. Architects from all sections of the country go to inspect this unique and marvelous piece of craftsmanship. When the work was completed and the Sister Superior of the convent wished to pay the man for his service, he was nowhere to be found. No one had seen him come or go. A reward was offered; no one ever claimed it. It is thought that the unknown carpenter was none other than St. Joseph, in whose honor the Sisters had communicated every Wednesday that he might assist them in erecting a staircase. There is no doubt that the prayers of those nuns were answered in a most remarkable way.

The building has subsequently been sold. Though no longer under the care of the Sisters of Loretto, it is still maintained and revered as a shrine.

On June 14, 1873, the Holy See declares that it does not approve the cultus of the "Heart of St. Joseph."

On May 11, 1878 the Holy See declared that if a statue of St. Joseph is not on the altar, it may be left uncovered in Passiontide.

Cap-de-la-Madeleine

Another example of St. Joseph deals with the Blessed Mother and construction of the great Canadian Shrine dedicated to the Blessed Mother at

Cap-de-la-Madeleine located at Three Rivers, Quebec. It was maintained by the Sisters of the Holy Name of Jesus and Mary whose foundress, Blessed Marie-Rose Durocher (1811–1849), was a relative of Blessed Brother André.

During the winter of 1878 to 1879, it was desired to build a larger church. Stone for this building was on the opposite side of the river. All hope to continue construction was lost when, during March, the river was no longer frozen. The saintly pastor, Fr. Luke Desilets, made a vow: "He would preserve the old church and dedicate it to the Holy Virgin if she would obtain a bridge of ice before the end of winter.

On March 14th and 15th some blocks of ice began to form and come together. Sunday, March 16th, the Vicar made a promise to the whole parish that a High Mass of Thanksgiving would be given in honor of St. Joseph on the morning of Wednesday, March 19th (St. Joseph's Feast Day) if they would be able to reach the other side of the river within a day. The first delivery of stones happened during the night of March 18th, at the hour when the priests commenced to say the office of St. Joseph. During the entire octave of the Feast of St. Joseph, they transported stone. The last journey was made on the Octave day itself. They then saw with amazement that the bridge of ice rapidly disengaged. Once again St. Joseph was there to assist his beloved bride.

The Apparition of Knock

We see yet another instance of St. Joseph's presence with the Blessed Mother. On August 21, 1879, the apparition of Our Lady of Knock took place. It all began about 7:00 P.M. There was something bright and luminous in the south gable of the chapel. It was a very dark night, raining heavily. Witnessed by numerous people was the apparition of the Blessed Mother, St. Joseph and St. John the Evangelist. The Blessed Virgin was life size while the other two were not quite as big, or as tall as Her figure. St. John had a book in his left hand and the index finger and middle finger of the right hand were raised as if he were speaking and impressing some point forcibly on the audience.

Though it was raining, the place where the figures appeared was quite dry. All this was observed by at least 18 witnesss. The apparition lasted until sometime past 9:00 P.M. The following is some of what the apparition at Knock has to teach us:

Mary wears a beautiful rose at Knock to tell us that she is Our Lady of the Rosary, Immaculate Mother of Grace and Mystical Rose. When we pray to Her, She wishes us to pray the rosary, and while doing so, to reflect upon the great mysteries of our faith.

The apparition of our Blessed Mother with St. Joseph and St. John the Evangelist helps to remind us of the mysteries of the rosary. St. Joseph reminds us of the Joyful Mysteries, our Lady reminds us of the Glorious Mysteries and St. John, beside the altar, the lamb and the cross, reminds us of the Sorrowful Mysteries.

The apparition at Knock brings before our eyes, St. Joseph, who is Patron of the Universal Church. He is symbolic of the working man and so represents the laity, the pilgrim people of God, whose duty it is to pay respect to Mary, their Queen and Mother. He gives us the example at Knock that we might do likewise. He reminds us of the very important role all lay people can play in the Church. As he was protector and guardian of the Church, so should all lay people defend, and speak for the Church at all times.

St. Joseph brings to our minds, thoughts of the mystery of the Word Incarnate, Jesus Christ made man.

We are led to reflect upon the life of the Holy Family of Nazareth. It should be our aim in life to imitate that life and so create in our world today, happy and holy families.

St. John, the beloved disciple of the Lord represents the hierarchy and the clergy. He is the link with the Church of today and the Church in the days of the Apostles.

Canon Antonio Vitali

Canon Vitali (1880–1885) said: "If the Church, ruling and ruled, teaching and taught, combined in a movement so general, and with such a transport of fervor, which may truly be called the work of the Most High, in rendering these great honors to St. Joseph, who can any longer doubt the primacy of Joseph over all the saints and angels? Who can henceforth separate him from Mary's side? Who can deny him a cultus, of dulia[8] it is true, but superior to that which is paid to any of the Blessed?"

"In order that Joseph, our most powerful patron, should intercede for us, for our families, for the Catholic Church, for the whole world, what remains for us to do? One thing for us, and one thing for our holy Mother, the Church. We, by true love to Jesus, by sincere devotion to Mary, by the practice of Christian Virtues, by filial tenderness and frequent exercises of piety towards Joseph, must render ourselves worthy of his special protection. All of whatever state or condition, must recognize him as their mirror, master, and leader, — princes, ecclesiastics, seculars, monarchs and subjects, pastors of souls and cloistered religious, priests and laymen, lettered men and artisans, virgins and married, young and old, men and women, rich and poor, — all must hold him as their particular advocate, for he has to protect all in life, in death, and after death, that is purgatory.... Then our Holy Mother the Church will certainly be neither reluctant nor slow to declare that Joseph is in glory and dignity superior, next to Mary, to all the angels and all the saints, thus placing Joseph in his true position, always and immediately close to his spouse, without exception, in the public prayers, sacred rites, and the Most Holy Sacrifice. Thus on the feasts of Mary, her dear spouse, Joseph, will ever be commemorated, and on the feasts of Joseph there will be a sweet memorial of Mary, even as fitly takes place on the feasts of the holy princes of the Apostles, Peter and Paul....

On September 19, 1883 Pope Leo XIII makes the Feast of St. Joseph an occasion when bishops are to officiate at Solemn Pontifical functions.

Leo XIII adds the Oration and other prayers after Mass on January 6, 1884, in which St. Joseph is invoked: "O God, our refuge and our Strength, etc."

During 1884 a change takes place regarding St. Joseph's Solemnity. As it held a double precept which would require abstention from servile work and obligatory attendance at Mass, it was a Holyday of obligation. March 19 was not made obligatory in the United States because the bishops felt the number of holydays should be kept to a minimum, since in a country so non-Catholic they were difficult to observe. An indult releasing March 19 from the Holydays of the Universal Church was granted by the Holy See to the III Plenary Council of Baltimore.

Also during 1884 the Leonine Prayers were decreed to be recited after all low masses and they incorporate a prayer that invokes St. Joseph among others.

There was a strong move among the Cardinals, Bishops, Clergy and laity to exalt the rank of St. Joseph in the Liturgical prayers of the mass second to Mary Immaculate by sending petitions to the Holy See. In 1887, 632 Bishops and Cardinals sent petitions for this purpose. Among them was the future Pope Pius X.

Quamquam Pluries

On August 15, 1889, Pope Leo XIII published *Quamquam Pluries,* which was the one major encyclical on St. Joseph. The actual text follows:

Although We have already ordered on several occasions that special prayers should be offered throughout the whole world and that Catholic interests should be recommended to God in a more earnest manner, let it not seem surprising to any one if at this time We judge that this duty should again be called to mind. In difficult times, especially when it seems that the powers of darkness are able to make daring attempts to ruin Christianity, the Church has always been accustomed to call humbly upon God, Her founder and champion, with greater earnestness and perseverance. In such times She has also sought aid from the saints who dwell in Heaven, especially the august Virgin Mother of God, whose patronage She, the Church, sees as a support in her trials. For the fruit of such pious prayers and of hope in the divine goodness will sooner or later become manifest.

Venerable Brothers, the present times are just as dangerous for Christian society as any dangerous periods of the past. We see very many people losing the faith which is the principle of all virtues. We notice charity going cold, we notice that youth are seduced by depraved manners and opinions on every side by violence and deceit, the Church of Jesus Christ is attacked on every side with violence and rage and an atrocious war has been waged against the papacy. The very foundations of religion are weakened by increasing violence every day. As for the depths of this catastrophe of our age and the ulterior schemes of the agitators, you yourselves know more than it behooves Us to put into words.

Amid such difficult and miserable conditions the evils of our day have grown too great for human remedies. It remains that the true healing of each of them is to be sought from the Divine Power. For this reason we have considered that we should arouse the piety of the Christian people to implore more zealously and constantly the help of the All-Powerful God. Indeed, with the approach of the month of October, which We elsewhere decreed should be dedicated to the Virgin Mary of the Rosary, We urgently exhort that during the present year the entire month be spent in the greatest possible devotion and piety. We have known how to appeal to the maternal goodness of the Virgin. We recognize that the hopes We have placed in Her are not in vain. If you reflect that She has always been present to the Christian commonwealth in times of need, can the heart doubt that She will renew the examples of power and grace if humble prayers are continually and perserveringly addressed to Her. Indeed so much the more wonderful we believe She has been, so much the more do we daily implore Her to continue this helpfulness.

But another proposal remains to be made, Venerable Brothers, well aware as We are that you will diligently cooperate with Us here as you have always done in the past. We think that God will help His Church as these prayers are joined with those of the Virgin Mother of God and Her most chaste spouse, St. Joseph. Accordingly, the Christian people are accustomed to implore this Virgin Mother of God and Her spouse, St. Joseph, with outstanding piety and trusting souls, which we have judged desirable and pleasing to the Virgin Herself.

In this matter, which We are publishing now for the first time, we recognize the popular piety, no longer quiet, but progressing along a well established course, namely the cult of St. Joseph which in former times the Roman Pontiffs strove to propagate widely and extensively. Finally in these times, We have seen that same veneration increased to such a point especially after Pius IXth of happy memory, Our Predecessor, declared the most Holy Patriarch, Patron of the Catholic Church, which he did at the request of very many bishops. But precisely because it is highly advantageous that veneration of St. Joseph be deeply rooted in Catholic morals and practices, We want to move and encourage the Christian people now especially, with our voice and our authority.

There are special reasons why Blessed Joseph should be explicitly named Patron of the Church and why it is very appropriate that the Church enjoy his protection and patronage. For he was the husband of Mary and father, as it was thought, of Jesus Christ. From this derives all of his dignity, grace, holiness and glory.

The dignity of the Mother of God is certainly so sublime that nothing can surpass it; but never the less, since the bond of marriage existed between Joseph and the Blessed Virgin, there is no doubt that more than any other person he approached that supereminent dignity by which the Mother of God is raised far above all the created things of nature.

For marriage is the closest possible union and relationship whereby each spouse mutually participates in the goods of the other. Moreover, if God gave Joseph as a spouse to the Virgin, he gave not only a companion of Her life, a witness of Her virginity, a defender of Her honor, but also, by that conjugal agreement God made him a partaker of Her lofty dignity.

Likewise, Joseph alone stands out in august dignity, because he was guardian of the Son of God and in the opinion of men was His father. As a consequence, the Word of God humbly subjected Himself to Joseph, and gave him every honor that children should render to their parents.

Therefore, from this double dignity there follow naturally the responsibilities which nature prescribes for the fathers of families, so that indeed, of the Divine House over which Joseph presided, he was the guardian, caretaker and legitimate and natural defender of duties and responsibilities he truly exercised throughout his mortal life with Supreme love and daily care. He strove to defend his spouse and the Divine offspring. He was accustomed to provide by his labor all daily food and everything necessary for the cultivation of both his wife and son. In seeking a place of refuge he warded off that danger blown out of the envy of the king. In the harsh difficulties of journeys and the inconvenience of exile, he was the perpetual companion, helper and consoler both of the Virgin and of Jesus.

Also, the Divine Home which Joseph governed with paternal authority, contained the beginning of the new Church. The Most Holy Virgin, as the Mother of Christ, is thus the Mother of all Christians. Indeed She brought them forth on the Mount of Calvary amidst the terrible sufferings of the Redeemer. And Jesus Christ, as the first born of Christians, who are His brothers by adoption and redemption. For these reasons, it is clear why the most Blessed Patriarch is recommended for a particular relationship to the multitude of Christians who constitute the Church as confided to his care in a certain special manner.

This is his numberless family, scattered throughout the world, over which he rules with a sort of paternal authority because he is the husband of Mary and the father of Jesus Christ. It is therefore agreeable and especially fitting for Blessed Joseph, that as he formerly served the Family of Nazareth in so many ways, so now by his heavenly patronage, Joseph guards and defends the Church of Christ.

Thus, Venerable Brothers, you easily understand from this, that many Fathers of the Church and of the Sacred Liturgy itself, agree to the opinion that ancient Joseph born of the patriarch Jacob foreshadowed the person and the duties of this, our Joseph.

And likewise showed forth with his own brilliance the greatness of the future guardian of the Holy Family. Indeed, besides, that both have the same name is not without significance. Rightly known to you are the other and brilliant likenesses between both Josephs. That former one received favor and singular benevolence from his lord and this same lord, the Pharaoh, placed him over his household and provided that prosperity came to the whole country through the favor of Joseph.

There was even a more evident similarity when by the king's order he was given supreme power over the entire kingdom. When calamity was brought by a deficient harvest and a scarcity of grain, he exercised charity, both for the Egyptians and the neighboring peoples, so that the king decreed that Joseph should be called the savior of the world. So also in that old patriarch it is legitimate to recognize the express image of this later patriarch, our Joseph. As the other brought prosperity and salvation to the members of the king's household and then wonderfully benefited the whole kingdom so also this later Joseph, destined for the guardianship of the Christian Name, must be reckoned to defend and protect the Church which truly is the House of the Lord and the Kingdom of God on earth.

This is why all peoples of every condition and place should recommend and entrust themselves to the faith and protection of Blessed Joseph. Fathers of families have in Joseph an outstanding form of vigilance and fatherly care. Spouses have in him a perfect specimen of love, of harmony and conjugal fidelity. Virgins have in him the same example and defender of virginal integrity, those of noble lineage can learn to preserve their dignity even under adverse circumstances. Let the wealthy understand what goods they should chiefly seek and earnestly amass. But also the needy, the laborers and all possessed of modest means should fly to his protection and learn to imitate him. For he, of royal blood, joined in holy matrimony to the greatest and holiest of all women; he was the father, as was thought, of the Son of God. Nevertheless, he devoted his life to labor and by his hands and skill produced whatever was necessary for those dependent on him.

Therefore, if truth be sought, the condition of those reduced to slender means is not disgraceful. The labor of craftsmen, far from being dishonorable, can by virtue be even greatly ennobled. Joseph, content on his own humble part with the difficulties of his vocation raised up his soul to the heights after the example of his own Son, who taking on the form of a servant, even though he was Lord of all, while entirely accepting supreme poverty and indigence.

Those who are poor should likewise feel and as many who seek their life for salaries or wages should raise up their thoughts and minds to improving their state and their need according to justice and ordering their lives according to the Providence of God, after the example of this Joseph. For to descend to violence and to undertake by sedition and disturbances in the name of justice is really foolishness. In most cases these produce only greater evils than those which they were meant to cure. Therefore, the poor should not entrust themselves to the promises of seditious men and they would not do so if they knew how to imitate the example and patronage of Blessed Joseph, and likewise the maternal charity of the Church which daily becomes more solicitous for their welfare.

And therefore, Venerable Brothers, we direct ourselves and our authority to your Episcopal duties which are not easy, but they are good, and pious and many. And as we have ordered, we decreed that you will spontaneously and voluntarily carry out what we have established, that throughout all of October in the recitation of the Rosary, the prayer to St. Joseph be added. The formula of which is sent to you with this letter. We decree that this order shall piously be observed in future years in perpetuity. To those who shall piously recite this prayer, We give an indulgence of seven years and seven times forty days for each recitation.

Salutary and deserving of highest commendation is the practice of consecrating the month of March by daily exercises of piety in honor of the Holy Patriarch. And where this is not able to be easily instituted, at least it is to be hoped that before his feast day, a tridium of prayers should be held in the principal church of each city. So that in every place where the 19th day of March, sacred to Blessed Joseph is not included among the number of Holydays of Obligation, we urge each of you that on that day in a holy manner out of private piety, so far as possible, you do not refuse to honor the Heavenly Patron in a manner as if it were a precept (a Holyday of Obligation).

And therefore, meanwhile, as an outstanding witness of Heavenly gifts and our benevolence to you, Venerable Brothers, and to your clergy and people, very lovingly in the Lord we impart the Apostolic Blessing.

Given at Rome at St. Peter's, the fifteenth day of August, the twelfth year of our Pontificate: Pope Leo XIII.

PRAYER to ST. JOSEPH for OCTOBER
(Assigned by His Holiness Leo XIII)

To you, O Blessed Joseph, we have recourse in our tribulations and having implored the help of your most holy Spouse, we confidently invoke your patronage also. By that love wherewith you were united to the Immaculate Virgin Mother of God, and by the fatherly affection with which you embraced the Child Jesus, we humbly pray you to look more graciously upon the inheritance which Jesus Christ purchased with His blood, and to assist us in our needs by your power and strength. O most watchful guardian of the Holy Family, protect the chosen people of Jesus Christ; keep far from us, most loving father, all blight of error and corruption; mercifully assist us from Heaven, most mighty defender, in our present conflict with the powers of darkness; and as of old you rescued the Child Jesus from the snares of the enemy and all adversity. Keep us one and all under your continual protection, in order that by your example and supported by your help, we may be enabled to lead a holy life, die a happy death, and come at last to possess eternal blessedness in Heaven. Amen.

Neminem Fugit

On June 14, 1892, Leo XIII calls on the Catholic world to honor and immitate the virtues of the Holy Family, often referring to St. Joseph as intimately related to Jesus and Mary. The following is the translation of *Neminem Fugit:*

It is a fact apparent to all that the welfare of the individual and of the state is in a special manner dependent on the family. Insofar as virtue has struck deep roots within the home and the character of children has been influenced in accordance with religious precepts by the teaching and example of parents, the common interest will be benefited. Consequently, it is of utmost importance, not only that the society of the home be established holily, but also that it be ruled by the holy laws, and that the spirit of religion and the standard of Christian living be diligently and steadfastly fostered there.

Hence, when God in His Mercy decided to carry out the work of man's redemption, so long expected through the centuries, He arranged to perform His task in such a way that in its beginnings it might show forth to the world the august spectacle of a Divinely founded family. In this, all men were to behold the perfect exemplar of domestic society, as well as of all virtue and holiness.

Such indeed was the family of Nazareth. In its bosom was concealed the Sun of justice, awaiting in anticipation the time when His full splendors should shine on all the nations — Christ our God, our Savior, together with His Virgin Mother and Joseph, that most blessed man, who exercised the rights of father over Jesus. We cannot doubt, then, that all the glories of domestic life, taking their origin in mutual charity, saintly character, and the exercise of piety, were without exception manifested in a superlative degree by the Holy Family as a pattern for all other families to imitate.

To this very end a benign providence had established the Holy Family, in order that all Christians in whatever walk of life or situation might have a reason and an incentive to practice every virtue, provided that they fix their gaze on the Holy Family. In Joseph, therefore, heads of the household are blessed with the unsurpassed model of fatherly watchfulness and care. In the holy Virgin Mother of God, mothers possess an extraordinary ideal of love, modesty, submission, and perfect loyalty. In Jesus, who "rendered them submission," children have before them the Divine picture of obedience to admire, venerate, and copy.

Let those who are nobly born, learn from this family of royal blood how to moderate their conduct in prosperity as well as to retain their self-respect in adversity. Let the wealthy understand how greatly virtue is to be preferred to riches. Workers, and all who are deeply embittered owing to reduced circumstances and a lowered standard of living, particularly in these times, will not lack reason for rejoicing over the lot that has befallen them rather than bewailing it, provided they will but turn their gaze on the blessed members of the Holy Family. In common with them they are subject to labor and with them they have their common cares of everyday life.

Joseph, too, was bound to find ways and means of wrestling a livelihood out of his earnings, while the very hands of God plied the tools of a carpenter. Nor, indeed, is there reason for us to wonder at those prudent men of affluence who in the past have wished to put away their wealth and to choose instead poverty with Jesus, Mary and Joseph.

When thus invoked, may Jesus, Mary and Joseph take their place in the family circle as its propitious patrons. May they foster charity, mould character and encourage the practice of virtue through imitation of their example; and by sweetening the burdens of this life which everywhere encompass us, may they render them more easy to bear.

Given at Rome, at St. Peter's under the seal of the Fisherman, June 14, 1892, the fifteenth year of our Pontificate.

Shortly after the publication of *Quamquam Pluries* (1889), the Sacred Congregation of Rites issued a decree discouraging further advances in the cultus of St. Joseph.

The author would like to note that this action of the Congregation of Sacred Rites indicated that the Holy See wished no changes at the time. The wording of the decree should be noted carefully. It does not criticize the soundness of the theological doctrine on which the petitions for St. Joseph's advancement rested. There is only the question whether or not a change at that time is expedient: "From all sides petitions have been sent to the Apostolic See, asking that St. Joseph be honored in the sacred liturgy with a cultus of higher rank. His Holiness was filled with the greatest joy because of these supplications which were presented to him . . . nevertheless he did not think to bestow on the Holy Patriarch a higher liturgical cultus which would alter the status wisely established in the Church over a long period."

The complete translation follows:

From the time that the Sovereign Pontiff, Pius IX, appointed Blessed Joseph, the most pure spouse of the Immaculate Mother of God and putative father of Jesus Christ, our Lord and Savior, Patron of the Whole Catholic Church, the ancient piety of Christians toward him, has wonderfully increased. Moreover this piety increased with a new flame, after our Most Holy Lord, Pope Leo XIII, by his encyclical letter under the date of August 15, 1889, celebrated the outstanding and very effective patronage before God of the glorious dignity of the same patriarch. The Pope has not hesitated to encourage and to promote devotion towards this holy patriarch by his exhortations and favors to the faithful. Hence, it happened that from all sides to this Apostolic See, there have been requests by which a cult of more ample dignity in the Sacred Liturgy should be given to Blessed Joseph. Moreover, his holiness is moved by the highest joy for these humble petitions brought to him as they report increasing devotion of the people daily, he considered that he should in no way enrich the same holy patriarch with a more outstanding liturgical cult which would change the order, already for a long time very wisely given to the most Holy Patriarch in the Church. But, since very often his Feast, fixed on March 19th, on account of the occurrance on Passion Sunday or during Holy Week, is unable to be celebrated on that day and hence its celebration according to the rubrics is sometimes extremely limited. Lest it turned to the detriment of that service which the whole Catholic world ought to exhibit for her Heavenly patron, His Holiness having consulted the Sacred Congregation of Rites determines in those years on which the aforesaid feast occur on Passion Sunday, the afore said Feast should be transferred to Monday immediately following, and as often as it will fall in Holy Week is transferred to Wednesday after the First Sunday after Easter as its proper place, preserving the prescriptions of the rubrics as regards the translation of feasts occuring on those days. Thus the Pope ordered this decree to be promulgated and to be added to the rubrics of the Breviary and the Roman Missal. On the day of August 15, 1892, Cardinal Aloisi-Masella, Prefect.

Theresa of Lisieux

Devotion to St. Joseph continues to abound. St. Theresa of Lisieux (1873–1897), a Carmelite nun, known as "the Little Flower of Jesus", maintained a great devotion to St. Joseph her entire life, specifically that of simplicity and trust. In her autobiography she wrote: "I prayed to St. Joseph to watch over me. From my childhood, my devotion to him was mingled with my love for the Blessed Virgin. Each day I recited the prayer: 'O St. Joseph, father and protector of virgins. . . !' It seemed that I was well protected and completely sheltered from every danger."

Her devotion was not sentimental, for she said of her mortifications, "I offered that which was sweet to the little Jesus, that which was difficult to St. Joseph." For a feast day celebration she composed the "Canticle to Our Father, St. Joseph."

Blessed Mother Katherine Drexel

As time progresses we find another "to be saint" who had great devotion to St. Joseph. On or about 1894 while on a trip to Virginia, Blessed Mother Katherine Drexel and Sister Mercedes arrived in Richmond at about 1:00 A.M. They had made no previous arrangements since they planned to spend the night at the train station. When they arrived they found the station closed. An elderly man approached and asked if they were the ladies the Sisters in Duval Street had sent him to meet. He took them to St. Joseph's Convent. On arriving at the convent, the man deposited their bags on the porch and left. Mother Katherine rang the door bell. The end result: finally gaining admittance, she realized no one was expecting them. Mother Katherine felt St. Joseph had intervened for their protection.

Blessed Brother André

That auspicious day back in 1845 marked the beginning for the apostle of St. Joseph. A child was born so frail that he was christened at the moment of his birth by the midwife. This child was Alfred Bessette who would be known as the "Miracle Man of Montreal" and would be responsible for the construction of St. Joseph's Oratory to be known as the "Lourdes of Canada." The next day Alfred was taken to the local church for a conditional baptism as the priest did not expect him to live.

As a note, Alfred Bessette was related to the foundress of the Grey Nuns, Saint Marguerite d'Youville (1701-1771) and Blessed Marie Rose Durocher (1811-1849), foundress of the Sisters of the Holy Names of Jesus and Mary, both on his maternal side. This may give an indication of what the future is to bring as Alfred Bessette would come to be known as Blessed Brother André, making for three saints in one family all having great devotion to Saint Joseph.

As a child he was nurtured in his faith by his mother. He remained a sickly child, unable to contribute to the household chores with his brothers and sisters.

Brother André is to suffer even more. On February 20, 1855, Br. André's father is killed while felling a tree. To add to the devastation for this young child, whose health is still very frail, on November 20, 1857, Br. André's mother dies. This leaves him in the nurturing hands of his aunt and uncle, Mr. and Mrs. Timothee Nadeau, in St. Césaire, S.E. of Montreal. At this time, shortly after his mother's death, he received his first Holy Communion from Fr. André Provençal. Fr. Provençal had a great devotion to St. Joseph, which he imbued in Br. André. His new family then left for the gold rush in California and Br. André is adopted by M. Louis Ouimet. During his stay with the Ouimet family, events occured which made him fearful of his faith and piety, therefore at the age of 15 he left St. Césaire for Farnham. This is the beginning of the wandering years of the orphan, who had been given a great devotion to St. Joseph by his mother, since his father was a carpenter like St. Joseph.

He next gains employment, as sexton, with Fr. Springer, the parish priest at Farnham. He finally has the opportunity of giving free rein to his piety.

At about 1863, Br. André migrated to the United States. During this period, the Civil War was at its peak. While alternating from the more healthful farm work and the more lucrative factory work, Brother André was able to learn to speak English, which would assist him in his future vocation.

After about four years in the States, Brother André returns to his homeland near Saint-Cesaire in 1867. At about this time Fr. André Provençal introduces Brother André to the Congregation of Holy Cross (c.s.c.). Br. André wanted some time to reflect on such a decision. Should he become a religious laybrother?

December 27, 1870 was a propitious day for St. Joseph as well as Brother André. Alfred Bessette officially took the name of Br. André (because of his great admiration for Fr. André Provençal) when he becomes a novice in the Congregation of Holy Cross. Br. André presents himself to the order with a letter from Fr. Provençal which stated "I am sending you a saint." Br. André was now destined to propagate the devotion to St. Joseph shortly after the official choice of St. Joseph as Patron of the Universal Church.

On January 8, 1872, the question regarding Br. André's health became a problem. There was some doubt whether he would be able to make his vows. With no other recourse, Br. André prevailed upon Bishop Bourget. Perhaps the Bishop had some presentiment of the future of this novice. With the desire for widespread devotion to St. Joseph which the Bishop had not as yet realized, he told Br. André he would make his vows. If nothing else, he could pray.

August 22, 1872 marked the date when Br. André made his first temporary vows and was officially named porter of Notre Dame College, a school for boys, maintained by the Congregation of Holy Cross, which was situated across the street from what was known as Mount Royal. As porter he had to answer the doorbell and look for the religious and students who were called to the parlor. In addition he woke the religious at 5:00 A.M. and rang the bell for various exercises always with strict punctuality. He was also responsible for keeping the parlor and three corridors neat and clean, went on errands and took care of the mail. On Mondays and Saturdays he drove to town for the students laundry. In odd hours he served as barber to the students, prepared the altar breads and made cinctures for the religious. All by a man with poor health.

Brother André made his perpetual vows February 2, 1874. As the work of Brother André proceeds, May 9, 1878 marked the publication of the first recorded testimony on five miracles attributed to the intercession of Brother André.

At this time Fr. Hupier was appointed Spiritual Director, who became a great comfort to Brother André. He was the one who introduced Brother André to St. Joseph's oil, which was an instrument Brother André used to ask St. Joseph's intercession to heal those of their afflictions.

Brother André was confident that St. Joseph wished to be honored on the land across from Notre Dame College, known as Mount Royal. Because of his devotion to St. Joseph, he was confident that the obstinate

Brother André at his Religious Profession (1874)

landlord would relinquish the land, thus sometime prior to 1890, Brother André had already concealed a medal of St. Joseph on the mountain.

During 1896 Brother Alderic, a companion of Brother André, buried a medal of St. Joseph on Mount Royal with anticipation of purchasing the land for St. Joseph. On July 22, 1896 the land, known as Mount Royal was purchased. They then cleared a path up the mountain which came to be known as "St. Joseph's Boulevard." In 1897 a small pavilion was built of rough hewn timber as a place to pray. A small statue and dish were placed so that the visitors might offer homage to St. Joseph and perhaps leave a few coins. Br. André's dream of a chapel to St. Joseph had not yet been realized but the foundation had been laid.

As the Nineteenth Century comes to a close, a new era in the cultus of St. Joseph has been encountered. After all the centuries, where St. Joseph was the silent saint, hidden in the lives of Jesus and Mary, he is now coming into his own, receiving the recognition that many have clamored for over the centuries.

---

[8] The homage paid to angels and saints.

CHAPTER NINE

The Twentieth Century begins with St. Joseph as Patron of the Universal Church. The Papacy now becomes far more vocal on devotion to St. Joseph. St. Joseph's time for recognition is coming.

Alexis H. M. Cardinal Lepicier

Alexis H. M. Cardinal Lepicier (1863–1936) wrote on St. Joseph the Helper. St. Joseph extends his powerful aid to all the faithful who turn to him, but there are some who benefit very particularly: those people, that is, whose condition or state in life gives them a certain likeness to him. In the first place, there are those who, longing to maintain a spirit of fervor in their hearts, gives themselves wholly to God's service by undertaking life under the vows of religion. It is by a natural instinct that such persons turn to Joseph with complete confidence, and receive through him the help that they need in order to persevere in the spirit of their exalted vocation.

St. Joseph is also the special patron of those who, experiencing the strong temptations of the flesh, wish nevertheless to live in continence, for the love of God and to keep up their religious devotion, against which the sin of impurity wages unremitting war. These too find effective help in their spiritual needs in this holy patriarch, guardian and father of virgins.

But it is especially at the hour of death that the reputed father of the Incarnate Word exerts his solicitous protection, he who himself was helped in that supreme moment by Jesus and Mary. He does not fail to ask God for the grace of a happy and holy death on behalf of those devout souls who trustfully call on him, for the grace that enables them to overcome the attacks of the Enemy, who at that critical moment does all he can to drive them to despair....

St. Joseph's aid is not confined to helping us in our spiritual needs; continual experience shows that he is no less eager to help in our temporal needs as well. We have only to look at the impressive generosity with which he comes to the assistance of the temporal good works which Christian charity never fails to produce in the Church. That, indeed, is one of the great wonders of our age — the countless charitable institutions that are born, that grow and increase, under the protection of this glorious patriarch....

St. Joseph's universal protection and help do not stop at the prayers he offers up for us before the throne of God and his promptness in thus coming to our aid. He exerts it furthermore through the pattern of virtue that he ceaselessly presents to our eyes, as the great Pope Leo XIII eloquently recalled.... Priests especially can find in St. Joseph's life examples of virtue fitting the holiness of their state, as the famous priest Frederick William Faber so well reminds us....

Finally it was again Leo XIII who reminded Catholics that every state and condition of life can find its model in St. Joseph: Fathers of families.... husbands and wives.... the highborn wealthy.... and especially the workers and other people of modest condition....

Pope Pius X wrote an epistle to Cardinal Lepicier regarding devotion to St. Joseph on February 12, 1908.

St. Joseph's Oratory

In 1862 the first sanctuary dedicated to St. Joseph in Montreal was founded by the Grey Nuns, while responding to the wishes of Bishop Bourget. The location of the sanctuary is now the present day Queen Elizabeth Hotel. This remained functional until

October 19, 1904 when it made way for St. Joseph's Oratory on Mount Royal. At this time Br. André's dream is coming to fruition. The first chapel measured 15 by 18 feet.

An interesting example of Divine Providence is the relationship between Bernadette of Lourdes and Br. André. Both were given their mission shortly after Church doctrine was declared. With her apparitions of the Blessed Virgin, her work was completed. Brother André had the power of miracles, yet his work would take twenty-five years for his mission to begin with the construction of the first Chapel dedicated to St. Joseph in 1904.

About 1907, Br. André originated the public Way of the Cross, which he led every Friday. The original Way of the Cross was laid out by Br. André with wooden crosses marking each station.

By 1908 the chapel needed to be enlarged and enclosed to accommodate the pilgrims. They also arranged for it to be heated in the winter. St. Joseph was receiving his recognition.

In 1909, the statue of St. Joseph and the Child was blessed for the Oratory by Pope Pius X. Today this is set in a niche at the far end of the Votive Chapel to the side of the Crypt Church. In the basin below the statue burns that which the pilgrims have come to know as St. Joseph's Oil.

During the Spring of 1909 Br. André is relieved, after 40 years service, of his duties as porter of Notre Dame College for boys and was made guardian of the Oratory.

Litany of St. Joseph

Pope Pius X approved and indulgenced the Litany of St. Joseph for public worship on March 18, 1909.

The Original Chapel of St. Joseph's Oratory in its mountain setting (1904)

Fr. Frederic

A person of great comfort to Br. André was a Franciscan priest, Fr. Frederic (1838–1916). He was born in France and in 1888 chose Trois-Rivieres for his new homeland. He is also remembered as one of three witnesses who saw the Madonna of the Cape open her eyes on June 22, 1888. He became a great friend of Br. André. Fr. Frederic would ask Br. André for his prayers, since he considered Br. André a great friend of St. Joseph.

According to the biography of Br. André, Fr. Frederic came in May 1911 "to the small Oratory of St. Joseph to verify Br. André's virtues. Remember dear Brother, that you are only the instrument of God for the wonders that St. Joseph is doing here. You must remain humble if you want the work here to prosper. Be always subject to your superiors and never undertake anything without their permission". Smiling Br. André took a small statue out of his pocket and said: "There is no danger, I have St. Joseph in the palm of my hand".

It must be noted that Br. André always displayed total humility and complete obedience to his superiors.

On the way down the hill, Fr. Frederic told the novices: "Brother André is truly a saint... You shall see marvelous things here".

Both men exhibited extreme humility as is shown on one meeting at the Oratory. On another occasion Fr. Frederic arrived at the Oratory and said: "I have come to ask Br. André what he is doing to become a great saint." The rector led him to the small chapel and ascended the stairs to Br. André's room. The latter came out to meet them. On seeing Br. André, the visitor fell on his knees, saying: "Give me your blessing, Br. André." "No, Fr. Frederic, it is you, rather, who should bless me." And there they were, each on his knees in a noble contest of humility.

On his deathbed, Fr. Frederic asked for Br. André, who brought him a medal of St. Joseph, promising to pray for a fast recovery. But Fr. Frederic replied: "Let God have His way." He died in Montreal. Fr. Frederic was beatified September 25, 1988.

Pope Pius X

On July 2, 1911 Pope Pius X declared that the Feast of St. Joseph may be celebrated on the First Sunday after March 19th. On July 24 of the same year it was declared that the Feast of March 19th is to be celebrated under the title "The Solemn Commemoration of St. Joseph, Spouse of the Blessed Virgin Mary," as a double of the first class. The Feast of the Patronage of St. Joseph is to be known as the "Solemnity of St. Joseph, Spouse of the Blessed Virgin Mary, Confessor, Patron of the Universal Church," on the Third Sunday after Easter as a double of the first class with a common octave.

On December 6, 1912, he declared that the Titular Feast of St. Joseph is to be celebrated on the Third Sunday after Easter.

On October 28, 1913, he advanced the Solemnity of St. Joseph from the Third Sunday after Easter to the Third Wednesday. March 19th is correspondingly reduced in rank to a double rite of the second class, although it is retained as a primary feast.

St. Joseph's Oratory

During 1914, Mr. Malenfont became a great help to Br. André and the Oratory. He felt that he needed to do something for God and lived by the philosophy "not to help others is to be useless. It is better to obey God than man." Guided by a dream in which he saw an old man trying to build a church and heard the old man calling him for help. He decided "this dream seems to be inspired by Heaven." To remove all his doubts in the matter he went in search of the old man who was asking for assistance. Though ridiculed, he felt he had a mission to perform, therefore he gave up all his earthly possessions and went to see Br. André in order to help with the construction of the Oratory.

He set out for Montreal. As he was climbing the path to the Oratory, he came upon the old man he had seen in his dream. Br. André said as he approached, "You are just the man I need." He thus began his wandering life for St. Joseph which he continued for ten years traveling to raise funds for St. Joseph and the Oratory.

Through Br. André's intercession to St. Joseph miraculous cures continued. There were 435 recorded during the year 1916.

Apparition at Fatima

Another example of St. Joseph in the lives of the saints and the life of the Blessed Mother is the Apparition at Fatima. August 13, 1917 was the scheduled date for the fourth apparition. The children were arrested by the local magistrate in order that they might explain the visions, therefore the apparition was unable to take place. The children were later released.

The children spent the day of August 19th as usual. In the afternoon they went to Valinhos. At about 4:00 P.M., Lucia began to recognize the signs of the apparition. When the apparition actually began, Lucia asked the Lady if she would be willing to perform a miracle so that all might believe. Our Lady answered: "Yes, in the last month, in October, I shall perform a miracle so that all may believe in My apparitions. If they had not taken you to the village, the miracle would have been greater. St. Joseph will come with the Baby Jesus to give peace to the world. Our Lord also will come to bless the people. Besides, Our Lady of the Rosary and Our Lady of Sorrows will come."

During the fifth apparition on September 13, 1917, Our Lady renewed the promises She had made during the last apparition.

The sixth apparition at Fatima was on October 13, 1917. The sun was now pale as the moon. To the left of the sun, St. Joseph appeared holding in his left arm the Child Jesus. St. Joseph emerged from the bright clouds only to his chest, sufficient to allow him to raise his right hand and make, together with the Child Jesus, the sign of the Cross three times over the world. As St. Joseph did this, Our Lady stood in all Her brilliancy to the right of the sun, dressed in the blue and white robes of Our Lady of the Rosary.

As Francisco and Jacinta were bathed in the marvelous colors and signs of the sun, Lucia was privileged to gaze upon Our Lord dressed in red as the Divine Redeemer, blessing the world, as Our Lady had foretold. Like St. Joseph, He was seen only from His chest up. Beside him stood Our Lady, dressed now in the purple robes of Our Lady of Sorrows, but without the sword. Finally, the Blessed Virgin appeared again to Lucia in all her ethereal brightness, clothed in the simple brown robes of Mount Carmel.

Our Lord already so much offended by the sins of mankind and particularly by the mistreatment of the children by the officials of the county, could easily have destroyed the world on that eventful day. However, Our Lord did not come to destroy, but to save. He saved the world that day through the blessings of good St. Joseph and the love of the Immaculate Heart of Mary for Her children on earth. Our Lord would have stopped the great World War then raging and given peace to the world through St. Joseph, Jacinta later declared, if the children had not been arrested and taken to Ourem. "What you do to these my least brethren," warns Our Lord, "You do to Me."

The Capucian Fathers talk of St. Joseph at Fatima by telling us there were 70,000 persons reassembled in the Valley of Iria, at Fatima to assist at the great miracle of the sun announced by the Virgin. During the forenoon it rained but behold at midday the rain ceased and the sun appeared. Right away, the sun began to spin and project on the ground all the colors of the spectrum.

During this time, the three children saw near the sun, the Virgin accompanied by St. Joseph and the Child Jesus. The virgin had promised in an earlier apparition that St. Joseph would come with the Child Jesus, giving peace to the world. St. Joseph with his fatherly hand, strong by the virtue of God, whom he carried on his arm, blessed the world three times.

Pope Benedict XV

Pope Benedict XV re-elevates March 19th to a high rank as a double of the first class. This was done on December 12, 1917.

On April 9, 1919, the Preface of St. Joseph is approved and assigned for use in all masses of St. Joseph.

Bonum Sane

Pope Benedict XV issued a special "Motu Proprio" on "St. Joseph and Labor" in commemoration of the Fiftieth Anniversary of the declaration of St. Joseph as Patron of the Church. The complete translation of *Bonum Sane* is as follows:

It was good and salutary indeed for the Christian commonwealth that our predecessor, Pius IX, of immortal memory, solemnly declared the most chaste spouse of the Virgin Mary and the foster-father of the Incarnate Word, St. Joseph, to be the Patron of the Universal Church. But now that the Fiftieth Anniversary of this happy event will occur next December, we consider it useful and opportune that it should be worthily celebrated by the whole Catholic world.

Casting our glance over the past fifty years, we behold the wonderfully flourishing conditions of pious institutions which bear witness to the manner in which devotion to the Holy Patriarch has been gradually developing among the faithful. When further, then, we consider the calamities afflicting the human race today, we cannot fail to realize how opportune it is to increase this devotion and spread it ever more widely throughout Christian peoples.

In our Encyclical, *On the reconciliation of Christian Peace,* following the cruel war, we indicated what was necessary to establish order and tranquility everywhere. In particular, consideration was given by us to the civil relations that exist between nations and between individuals. Yet today the treatment of another cause of disturbance, much more serious, becomes imperative. There is question now of an evil that has crept into the very heart of society. For the scourge of war had been laid on the human race at the very moment it had become profoundly infected with naturalism — that great worldly plague which, wherever it enters, lessens the desire of heavenly things, extinguishes the flame of Divine Love, and deprives man of the healing and elevating grace of Christ, leaving him without the light of faith, dependent on the weak and corrupt resources of nature and the slave of unbridled human passion.

Thus it happened that many devoted themselves solely to the acquisition of worldly goods. Moreover, while the contest between the wealthy and the proletariat had already become acute, class hatred now became still more grave by reason of the length and severity of the war, for while this on the one hand brought intolerable privation to the masses, on the other it rapidly made fortunes for the few.

Then, too, the holiness of conjugal fidelity and respect for paternal authority were often grievously transgressed during the war. The remoteness of one spouse served to relax the bond of duty to the other. And the absence of a watchful eye gave rise to freer and more indulgent conduct. More particularly was this notable among younger women. Sincerely to be regretted, therefore, is the fact that public morals have become far more corrupt and depraved than they had previously been, and for this very reason, too, the so called "social question" has reached an intensity which causes one to fear the gravest of evils.

In the wishful thinking and expectations of the seditious members of society there has consequently been maturing the advent of a certain universal commonwealth that is to be founded on absolute equality of men and on community of goods. National distinctions are no longer to exist in this, nor is any recognition to be given to the authority of the father over his sons, of public power over the citizens, or of God over men united in civil commonwealth. All such ravings, should they be carried into effect, must culminate in a tremendous social convulsion, such in fact as is now experienced and felt by not a small part of Europe. Precisely a similar condition of affairs, we are aware, is ambitioned among other peoples. The masses are wrought into excitement by the fury and audacity of a few, while grave disturbances break out in many places.

Meanwhile, preoccupied above all else with this course of events, we have not failed to renew in the sons of the Church a sense of their duty, whenever the occasion presented itself. This purpose, for example, we but recently accomplished through the letter addressed by us to the Bishop of Bergamo and also to the bishops of the Venetian Province. And so now, prompted by the same motive, namely to recall to their duty those of our own fold, however many, who earn their bread by labor of their hands, and to preserve them immune from the contagion of socialism, that which nothing is more opposed to Christian wisdom, we have with great solicitude placed before them in a particular manner the example of St. Joseph, that they may follow him as their special guide and may honor him as their heavenly patron.

It was he, who in every deed lived a life similar to theirs, and for this reason Our Lord Jesus Christ, though in truth, the Only-begotten Son of the Eternal Father, wished to be called the "Son of the Carpenter." Yet how numerous and how great were the virtues with which he adored his poor and humble condition! Among all these virtues none was wanting to ennoble the man who was to be the husband of Mary Immaculate and to be thought the father of Our Lord Jesus Christ.

Let all persons, then, learn from Joseph to consider present passing affairs in the light of the future good which will endure forever, and find consolation amid human vicissitudes in the hope of heavenly things, so that they may aspire to them in a manner conformable to the Divine Will — that is, by living soberly, justly and piously. In reference to the labor problem it is opportune to quote here the words which our predecessor, Leo XIII of happy memory uttered on this question, for they are such that no ther words can be considered appropriate.

With the increase of devotion to St. Joseph among

the faithful there will necessarily result an increase in their devotion toward the Holy Family of Nazareth, of which he was the august head, for these devotions spring spontaneously one from the other. By St. Joseph we are led directly to Mary, and by Mary to the fountain of all holiness, Jesus Christ, who sanctified the domestic virtues by his obedience toward St. Joseph and Mary.

We desire, then, that these marvelous exemplars of virtue should serve as inspiration and as models for all Christian families. Even as the family constitutes the foundation of the human race, so by strengthening domestic society with the bonds of purity, fidelity and concord, a new vigor and new lifeblood will be diffused through all the members of human society under the vivifying influence of the virtue of Christ; nor shall the result consist merely in the correction of public morals but in the restoration of public and civil discipline itself.

Therefore, full of confidence in the patronage of him to whose providence and vigilence it pleased God to entrust His Only-begotten Son as well as the Virgin Most Holy, we earnestly exhort all the bishops of the Catholic world that in the Church's present need they should induce the faithful to implore more earnestly the powerful intercession of St. Joseph. And since there are many ways approved by this Apostolic See for venerating the Holy Patriarch, especially on all Wednesdays of the year and during the month consecrated to him. We wish that at the insistance of each bishop all these devotions should be practiced in each diocese as far as possible.

Then, too, since Joseph, whose death took place in the presence of Jesus and Mary, he be justly regarded as the most efficacious protector of the dying, it is our purpose here to lay a special injunction on our Venerable Brethren that they assist in every possible manner those pious associations which have been instituted to obtain the intercession of St. Joseph for the dying — such as the *Association for a Happy Death,* and the *Pious Union of St. Joseph's Passing,* established for the benefit of those who are in their last agony...

Given at St. Peter's in Rome, July 25, Feast of St. James the Apostle, 1920, in the sixth year of our Pontificate.

An invocation in honor of St. Joseph is inserted by Pope Benedict XV in the Divine Praises: "Blessed be St. Joseph, Her most chaste spouse." This was presented February 23, 1921.

On August 9, 1922, the invocation of St. Joseph is ordered to be included in the special prayer for the moment of death.

St. Joseph's Oratory

As the growth of St. Joseph's Oratory continues, December 16, 1917 marked the opening and the blessing of the Stone Crypt Church, which could seat 1000.

In May, 1921, a rally was organized by the Knights of Columbus. 3400 Knights succeeded in gathering 25,000 people under the supervision of James A. Flaherty, Supreme Knight, for an afternoon at the Oratory with Brother André.

August 31, 1924 marks the blessing of the cornerstone and the start of construction of the large basilica on Mount Royal. Br. André's monument to St. Joseph is becoming a reality.

Allocution Praising Joseph

April 22–23, 1926 was the date for the Allocution of Pius XI, praising St. Joseph. The complete translation is as follows:

Brother André at the age of 75 (1920)

Here is a saint who enters the world and spends his life in fulfilling the most exalted mandate from God, the incomparable mission of guarding the purity of Mary, of protecting the divinity of Jesus Christ, a knowing cooperator in preserving the secret unknown to all except the most Blessed Trinity, that of the Mystery of the Redemption of the human race. And it is in the grandeur of this mission that the singular and absolutely incomparable holiness of St. Joseph lies, because truly such a great mission was not confided to any other soul, to any other saint, and thus, between Joseph and God we do not see nor can we see anyone except the most Holy Mary with Her Divine Maternity. It is evident that in such an exalted mission this saint already possessed title to the glory which is his, the glory of Patron of the Universal Church. The whole Church was, in fact, there beside him, like a seed already fecundated, in the humanity and in the blood of Jesus Christ; the whole Church was there in the virginal Motherhood of the Most Holy Mary, Mother of Jesus and the Mother of all the faithful, who at the foot of the Cross were to become Her children in the blood of Her first-born son, Jesus. What a small thing in human eyes, but what a great thing in the spiritual view: the Church was already there with St. Joseph when he was in the Holy Family, the guardian, the protecting father.

Confidence in St. Joseph

During 1926, the Italian St. Joseph Orphanage was maintained by the Compassionate Servants of Mary. The direction of the orphanage was given to the religious women. The Superior then remarked "with St. Joseph, all will come out well." Devotion to St. Joseph, held in honor at the orphanage, was indeed engraved in the hearts of the little orphans; this is a fact which they asked often of their parents on days of reunions when they asked their parents to bring them to the Oratory. When they would prepare their vocation, a novena to St. Joseph was made with devotion. Several would go to the Oratory on the day of their marriage so that St. Joseph continued to protect them in the new life for which they were commencing.

Brother André's Solution

In conjunction with keeping the Holy Family as one entity, the following is an example of Brother André's advice. In May of 1927 an epidemic of typhoid fever struck Montreal. Many of the sick were treated at Sacred Heart Hospital in Cartierville, staffed by the Sisters of Providence. Four of the nuns who nursed the sick ended up with the fever. The Superior of the hospital feared for the other nuns. The Superior called on Sr. LeBlanc (a confidant for some time of Br. André) and asked her to bring Br. André to intercede.

Br. André had his formula: set up an altar in the center of the hospital, with a statue of our Lady of Sorrows, and carry the statue in procession through the hospital. Since he did not want to divide the spouses of Nazareth, the following Wednesday he placed a statue of St. Joseph on the altar and held a procession. Meanwhile the sisters would visit the Blessed Sacrament and do the Stations of the Cross. With so much input from Heaven, Br. André's word came true: the sick nuns were cured and no other nun caught typhoid.

Allocution by Pope Pius XI

Pope Pius XI gave another allocution on March 19, 1928. The complete translation is as follows:

Between these two missions (of John the Baptist and St. Peter) there appears the mission of St. Joseph, withdrawn, silent, almost unperceived, destined to shine forth only several centuries later — a silence which was to be followed no doubt by a resounding chant of glory, but long, long afterward. Indeed, there, where the mystery is more profound, where the shades of night covering it are more dense, where the silence is more complete, truly there it is that the mission is more exalted and the ensemble more brilliant of the requisite virtues and of the merits called on by happy necessity to be their echo. This was a unique and magnificent mission, that of protecting the Son of God and King of the world; the mission of protecting the virginity and holiness of Mary; the singular mission of entering into participation in the great mystery hidden from the eyes of past ages, and of thus cooperating in the Incarnation and in the Redemption. The whole sanctity of St. Joseph consists precisely in the scrupulously faithful accomplishment of this mission so great and so humble, so exalted and so hidden, so splendid and so surrounded by darkness.

St. Joseph's Hypostatic Union

The allocution by Pope Pius XI, dated March 19, 1935, on St. Joseph's Hypostatic Union. The complete translation is as follows:

This is the mystery, the secret of the Divine Incarnation, of the Redemption, which the Holy Trinity reveals to man. In truth, it is impossible to rise higher. We are in the order of the Hypostatic Union, of the personal union of God with man. It is in this moment that the gesture of God invites us to consider the humble and great saint; it is in this moment that God utters the word which explains all the relationships between St. Joseph and all great prophets and all the great saints, even those who have had elevated public missions like the Apostles. No other distinction can surpass that of having received the revelation of the Hypostatic Union of the Divine Word. . . . The source of every grace is the Divine Redeemer; after him there is Mary, the dispensatrix of the Divine Graces. But if there is anything that should arouse still greater confidence on our part, it is, in a certain way, the thought that St. Joseph is the one who is able to do everything, along with the Divine Redeemer and his Divine Mother, and in a manner and with an authority which surpasses that of mere minister and guardian. . . . in the case of Jesus and Mary, the angels offer them respect and veneration. And in their turn, Jesus and Mary themselves obey and offer their homage to Joseph, for they reverence what the hand of God has established in him, namely, the authority of spouse and the authority of father. Consequently, our confidence in this saint should be great, founded as it is on such prolonged and even unique relationships with the very sources of grace and of life, the Blessed Trinity.

Petitions in favor of St. Joseph

Even more enthusiasm was brought forth for the cultus of St. Joseph in 1935. A petition signed by 40,000 people from Germany, Austria and German communities of Canada and the United States was sent to the Holy See. Another petition signed by 100,000 faithful supported by the petition of their pastor Msgr. M. Phelan of St. Joseph's parish Capitola, California was sent. The contents of these petitions were that St. Joseph being the Patron of the Universal Church was to be given a place of importance next to the sweet name of Mary in the prayers of the supreme sacrifice of the mass, namely in the Confiteor, Suspice Sancta Trinitas, Communicantes of the canon and Libranos.

The flimsy objections which were brought forward

against these petitions were (1) that St. Joseph died before our Lord performed His Supreme sacrifice of His life on the cross at Calvary and therefore it was not fit to include his name in the mass prayers. (2) In 1939 the objection raised by the spokesmen against the change was that the Church did not wish to tamper with the long standing traditions of the mass prayers. If a devout soul is to examine the history of the Church in relation to St. Joseph it becomes clear that although St. Joseph was not given due honors in the mass during the early period, it has now become a recognized fact that St. Joseph is now to be venerated next to Mary, his most chaste spouse.

St. Joseph's Oratory

St. Joseph's Oratory faced a new obstacle. On the First Wednesday of November 1936, since the construction of the Basilica had been halted because of the lack of funds, the council at the Oratory asked Brother André whether construction should be abandoned. Br. André suggested that a statue of St. Joseph be placed in the unfinished walls of the Basilica, saying "if St. Joseph wants a roof over his head, he will find a way to provide it."

12:50 A.M. on January 6, 1937, Brother André died. During seven days, more than a million persons passed by his bier. Day and night the Oratory was inundated with pilgrims wanting to pay there respects to Br. André. He was given the acclaim usually reserved for Pontiffs or dignitaries.

On Atheistic Communism

St. Joseph is named the Guardian of the spiritual battle against communism by Pope Pius XI on March 19, 1937. The encyclical was titled *On Atheistic Communism*. The complete translation follows:

To hasten the advent of the Peace of Christ in the Kingdom of Christ, so ardently desired by all, we place the vast campaign of the Church against world communism under the standard of St. Joseph, Her mighty protector. He belongs to the working-class, and he bore the burdens of poverty for himself and the Holy Family, whose tender and vigilant head he was. To him was entrusted the Divine Child when Herod loosed his assassins against Him. In a life of faithful performance of everyday duties he left an example for all those who must gain their bread by the toil of their hands. He won for himself the title the "Just Man," serving thus as a living model of that Christian justice which should reign in social life.

October 1937 marks the date when the dome of the basilica towered over Mount Royal in Montreal (later to be known as the largest shrine in the world dedicated to St. Joseph). Almost a year to the day, the work was accomplished that Br. André said St. Joseph would complete. As 1937 comes to a close we look to the great developments of St. Joseph's devotion. Br. André's work has been accomplished yet we will find that there is so much more to be done. As he said on his deathbed, "How much more I can do in Heaven."

CHAPTER TEN

We continue the Twentieth Century with the further development of devotion to St. Joseph.

Omnipotent Intercession

Pope Pius XI alludes to the *Omnipotent Intercession* of St. Joseph in his letter of March 19, 1938. The full translation is as follows:

The august Pontiff could not wish for his children anything truer, richer, more full of the promise of every grace and prosperity, than to pray that their homes be like the family presided over truly by St. Joseph with the authority of a father, and to ask that this protector of the family to which Mary and Jesus belonged be also the great patron of their homes. May St. Joseph by his paternal providence and his omnipotent intercesion be always ready to help their homes and their own persons! It is customary to reserve this use of omnipotent to the intercession of Mary, but he dares to say that it should also be applied to St. Joseph. Actually, the intercession of Mary is that of the mother, and consequently, we do not see how Her Divine Son could refuse anything to such a mother. But the intercession of St. Joseph is that of the husband, the putative father, the head of the Holy Family of Nazareth which was composed of himself, Mary and Jesus. And as St. Joseph was truly the head or the master of that house, his intercession cannot be but all-powerful. For what could Jesus and Mary refuse to St. Joseph, he who was entirely devoted to Them all his life, and to whom They truly owed the means of Their earthly existence?

Assumption of the Blessed Virgin

November 1, 1950 marked the official definition by the Church of the Assumption of the Blessed Virgin Mary as dogma of the Catholic Church. Yet all true Christians believed it for centuries. Why, then should we not believe in the resurrection and assumption of St. Joseph for which there are so many convincing reasons.

Joseph the Worker

Pope Pius XII institutes the Feast of "St. Joseph the Worker" on May 1, 1955, replacing the Solemnity of St. Joseph and to compete with the Communists celebration of May Day. The complete translation of *Joseph the Worker* follows:

From the beginning we put your organization under the powerful patronage of St. Joseph. Indeed, there could be no better protector to help deepen in your lives the spirit of the Gospel. As we said then (March 11, 1945), that Spirit flows to you and to all men from the heart of the God-man, Savior of the world, but certainly, no worker was ever more completely and profoundly penetrated by it than the foster-father of Jesus, who lived with him in closest intimacy and community of family life and work. Thus, if you wish to be close to Christ, we again today repeat, "Go to Joseph" (Gen. 41:44).

Yes, beloved workers, the Pope and the Church cannot withdraw from the Divine mission of guiding, protecting and loving especially the suffering, who are all the more dear, the more they are in need of defense and help, whether they be workers or other children of the people. This duty and obligation we, the Vicar of Christ, desire to declare again clearly here on this first day of May, which the whole world of labor has claimed for itself as its own proper feast day. We intend that all may recognize the dignity of labor, and that this dignity may be the motive in founding the social order and the law founded on the equitable distribution of rights and duties.

Acclaimed in this way by Christian workers and having received, as it were, Christian Baptism, the first day of May far from being an incitation to discord, hate and violence is and will be a recurring invitation to modern society to accomplish what is still lacking for social peace. A Christian feast, therefore, that is a day of rejoicing for the concrete and progressive triumph of the Christian ideals of the great family of all who labor.

In order that this meaning may remain in your minds and that in some way we may make an immediate return for the many and precious gifts brought to us from all parts of Italy, we are happy to announce to you our determination to institute as in fact we do now institute the liturgical feast of St. Joseph the Worker, assigning it to the first day of May. Are you pleased with this our gift, beloved workers? We are certain that you are, because the humble workman of Nazareth not only personifies before God and the Church the dignity of the man who works with his hands, but he is always the provident guardian of you and your families.

Patronage of St. Joseph

Echoing the week of studies held at St. Joseph's Oratory of Montreal during August 1 to 9, 1955. The Canadian Episcopate decreed 1955 the year of St. Joseph to commemorate the 85th anniversary of the proclamation by Pius IX of St. Joseph as Patron of the Universal Church and the 50th anniversary of the foundation of St. Joseph's Oratory. These memorable occasions called for such a manifestation.

From October 7 to 14, 1945 at the celebrated sanctuary of Barcelona, San José de Montaña (St. Joseph of the Mountains) six conferences on St. Joseph had been pronounced, of which one by Canon Alastruey, the Dean of the Theological faculty of the University of Salamanca and the Mariologists of renowned, is significant. Hardly a month later from November 24–30 of the same year, a dozen people came together for a conference in Mexico. This time treating the principle points of theology about St. Joseph to appreciate his titles as Spouse of Mary and Foster-father of Jesus, his supereminent sanctity and his role of patron. The following year Spain drew the attention of theologians. The Discalced Carmelites held at Valladolid an important week of studies which had as a result the official launching of the first scientific review of Josephology under the title "Estudios Josefinos". Among the dozen works presented there the more remarkable treated in masterful fashion the fundamental points of the theology of St. Joseph.

Finally, the Iberian-American Society of Josephology organized, in 1951, a week of studies on the Fatherhood of Saint Joseph and a second in 1954 on the Marriage of the Holy Virgin and St. Joseph.

His Eminence Cardinal Leger deemed to pronounce the opening sermon explaining in prophetical fashion the chosen place which belongs to St. Joseph in the mystical body of Christ.

The persons giving conferences undertook also a complete exposition of the teaching of the Fathers of the Church about the Patronage of St. Joseph. Some of them attempted a special work about St. Joseph as patron of workers or as Patron of Mission Lands or still as Patron of the Anti-Communist struggle. Naturally as Patron of Workers he would be interested in a correct organization of working people.

As Mary's spouse, Joseph is the Universal Patron for all material and spiritual needs for all classes of society, for all states of life. Like her, he is a very efficacious and even all powerful according to the very strong and clear words of Pius XI. He exercises an empire of rule, of love over the heart of Mary and Jesus and indeed over the heart of God. Now this doesn't signify that St. Joseph is on a level of equality with the Holy Virgin. The universal mediation of Mary is in strict and constant subordination with that of her Son and its He who furnishes her value and its efficacy. The same is true of St. Joseph. He draws his greatness and his power from his intimate and perpetual dependence on that of Jesus and of Mary. So here we have the earthly Trinity which continues in Heaven in an admirable union, continuing its work of love and doing good.

Statue of St. Joseph with Child Jesus

On August 9, 1955, the statuette of St. Joseph and the Child was crowned by His Eminence Paul-Emile Cardinal Leger acting as Papal Legate on authority of the Holy See. This is the statue found in the Votive Chapel at the Oratory in Montreal.

Address to American School Children

Pope Pius XII gave a radiocast to the American school children on February 19, 1958, on the virtues of St. Joseph. The complete translation follows:

Is it possible that another Lent has come around and that we are asked once again to speak to our dear school children in America? Surely nothing pleases us more than to talk with the young ones of the cherished flock belonging to the Divine Shepherd. During the year hundreds and hundreds of children come to

Crowned statue of Saint Joseph with the Child Jesus (1955)

see us here in Rome and out in the hill country nearby. We talk to them and often they answer our questions. We cannot do that this morning, because you are too far away. But at least our voice can travel across the ocean, and in one way bring us really into your classrooms.

And what is the message it carries for you? Let us tell you briefly. Next week you will begin the month of St. Joseph. Now we have decided this year to entrust to him the charge of all we fondly wish and hope for from you.

St. Joseph, as you have all learned at home and at school, was a very holy man. He had to be, because he was married to the Virgin Mary, the purest, the holiest, the most exalted of all God's creatures. More than that, the eternal father confided to the care of St. Joseph His own Only-begotten Son, became man on earth, Jesus Christ. Mary was the mother of Jesus, the tenderest and most loving of all mothers; and though Joseph was not His father, he had for Him by a special gift from heaven all the natural love, all the affectionate solicitude that a father's heart can know. With Mary his wife, he shared all the joys and sorrows, the plans and anxieties that come to a mother in bringing up her child. Day after day, at home and in the carpenter shop, his eyes rested on Jesus; he protected him against the dangers of childhood; he guided his advancing years, and by hard work and with religious devotedness he provided for the increasing needs of the Mother and the Son.

What a beautiful family life there was at Nazareth! You call it the Holy Family, and rightly so. In that small house you find Jesus, holy more than anyone can imagine, who has come to help you and everybody become holy and pleasing to the Father. There you find His mother, your blessed Mother; and, as you know, from the first breath She breathed and all during the days of Her life, Her soul was simply one marvelous, indescribable thing of beauty, like a precious jewel whose every facet reflected clearly, unobstructed, the infinite holiness of God. And then there was Joseph, modest, self-effacing, yet exercising authority over the family. How holy he must have been! Under his fatherly protection and ceaseless, timeless care, the young boy grew into manhood, who later on Calvary's Cross, dying would restore life to man, and draw all men into oneness through grace with Himself. With him as their head they should then form that one big, big family scattered all over the world. You call that family the Church, the one, true Catholic Church, of which you are members, and that membership is your richest treasure on earth.

Now let us ask you dear children, if Joseph was so engaged heart and soul in protecting and providing for that little family at Nazareth, don't you think that now in Heaven he is the same loving father and guardian of the whole Church, of all its members, as he was of its head on earth? We hear your answer: Yes. And does he not know that, Oh so many of its children are terribly in need of help? They need help for their souls — the grace of repentance, the grace of perseverance, the grace of humble, unstinted surrender to the Holy Will of God; and Joseph turns to Jesus, of old, his boy of Nazareth, and at once graces flow abundantly for the souls of men.

They need help also for their bodies: fathers are out of work, mothers are bending beneath burdens far too heavy, children are without sufficient food and clothing and medicines when ill; and Joseph turns to you. Yes, it is to you he turns. He must look to you to aid and encourage those children, who are also your little brothers and sisters. We know you will not fail him.

Your devotion to him will spur you on to make little sacrifices and big ones, too, so that the vast human family that Jesus yearns to unite in faith and charity, will know that St. Joseph is still the alert and generous guardian and protector, working now through his loyal clients. And so as we said at the beginning, with confidence we commit to him the charge to bestir the unselfish affection that fills your hearts for those who need and ask assistance.

We leave you now, dear children, but first we wish to give you a proof of the fatherly care we have for all of you. And so, with the full affection of our heart we impart to you, to your dear parents, and all at home, to your teachers and pastors, our Apostolic Benediction. May it draw down into your souls the strong grace of abiding fidelity to God and his Church; and never forget that St. Joseph is always standing by to protect you.

CHAPTER ELEVEN

Pope John XXIII

Pope John XXIII was Pope from 1958 to 1963. During that time he spoke quite extensively on St. Joseph, petitioning the faithful to enrich their devotion to St. Joseph. For those without the devotion, he asked them to make it part of their devotional life.

The first of his many letters was an allocution on the virtues of St. Joseph on March 19, 1959. The complete text follows:

All the saints in glory assuredly merit honor and particular respect, but it is evident that St. Joseph possesses a just title to a more sweet, more intimate and penetrating place in our hearts, belonging to him alone. . . . Here we are able to estimate completely all the greatness of St. Joseph, not only by reason of the fact that he was close to Jesus and Mary, but also by the shining example he has given of all virtues. . . . St. Joseph is the outstanding protector of the family, along with the other two persons whose incomparable guardian he was. The mere mention of Jesus, Mary and Joseph reminds us that here we find all human history; here is summed up all the saving action, the grandeur, the beauty, the splendor of the Catholic Church.

Bishop Fulton J. Sheen

Bishop Fulton J. Sheen (1895–1979) wrote eloquently on the *Love of Joseph and Mary* in the following article published in 1961 from *The World's First Love*. The following are his words:

Joseph was probably a young man, strong, virile, athletic, handsome, chaste and disciplined; the kind of man one sees sometimes shepherding sheep, or piloting a plane, or working at a carpenter's bench. Instead of being a man incapable of loving, he must have been on fire with love. Just as we would give very little credit to the Blessed Mother if she had taken her vow of virginity after having been an old maid for fifty years, so neither could we give much credit to a Joseph who became her spouse because he was advanced in years. Young girls in those days, like Mary, took vows to love God uniquely, and so did young men, of whom Joseph was one so pre-eminent as to be called the *just*. Instead, then, of being dried fruit to be served on the table of the King, he was rather a blossom filled with promise and power. He was not in the evening of life but in its morning, bubbling over with energy, strength and controlled passion.

Mary and Joseph brought to their espousals, not only their vows of virginity, but also two hearts with greater torrents of love than had ever before coursed through human breasts. No husband and wife ever loved one another so much as Joseph and Mary. . . Love usually makes husband and wife one. In the case of Mary and Joseph, it was not their combined loves but Jesus who made them one. No deeper love ever beat under the roof of the world since the beginning, nor will it ever beat, even unto the end. They did not go to God through love to one another; rather, because they went first to God, they had a deep and pure love one for another. . .

How much more beautiful Mary and Joseph become when we see in their loves what might be called the first *Divine Romance!* . . . In both Mary and Joseph, there was youth, beauty and promise. God loves cascading cataracts and billowing waterfalls, but he loves them better, not when they overflow and drown flowers, but when they are harnessed and bridled to light a city and to slake the thirst of a child.

In Joseph and Mary, we do not find one controlled waterfall and one dried-up lake, but rather two youths who, before they knew the beauty of the one and the handsome strength of the other, willed to surrender these things for Jesus.

Le Voci

On March 19, 1961, John XXIII issued a document of great importance for the cause of St. Joseph. This Apostolic Letter announced the selection of St. Joseph as heavenly protector of the Second Vatican Council. The complete translation of *Le Voci* follows:

VENERABLE BRETHREN AND BELOVED CHILDREN!

The expressions which have come to Us from every corner of the earth stir Us to draw profit from the good dispositions of so many open and sincere hearts, who joyously wait for the Second Ecumenical Council of the Vatican and hope for its successful outcome. With loving spontaneity they devote themselves to beg heavenly aid. They turn toward increased religious fervor, toward a clearer understanding of all that the celebration of the Council will require beforehand and will subsequently produce in the form of increasing the interior and social life of the Church and the spiritual renovation of the entire world.

And now, as a new spring appears and we stand on the threshold of the sacred Easter liturgy, we find ourselves face to face with the gentle and kind figure of St. Joseph, the august spouse of Mary — one so dear to those souls most responsive to the attractions of Christian asceticism and to expressions of religious devotion that are reserved and modest but all the sweeter and more pleasing for being so.

In the Church's cult, Jesus, the Word of God made man, received from the beginning the adoration which is due Him as the splendor of the substance of the Father, a splendor reflected in the glory of the saints. Mary, His mother, followed Him closely ever since the first centuries, piously venerated in the images of the catacombs and basilicas as "Holy Mary, Mother of God." Joseph, however, except for certain sporadic appearances which are found here and there in the writings of the fathers, for long centuries remained in his characteristic obscurity, like a kind of ornamental detail in the picture of the Savior's life. Time had to pass before his cultus passed from passing glances to the hearts of the faithful, then to surge forth in a special movement of prayer and trusting confidence. Such fervent joy was reserved for the outpourings of our modern day; Oh! How rich and imposing have they been! We are particularly happy to collect from them certain observations that are at once quite characteristic and significant.

St. Joseph in the Words of the Pontiffs of the Last Hundred Years

Among the various petitions which the Fathers of the First Vatican Council presented to Pius IX during their meeting in Rome (1869–70), the first two concerned St. Joseph. The first asked that his cultus might be accorded a higher place in the sacred Liturgy. The second asked for the solemn proclamation of St. Joseph as Patron of the Universal Church.

Pius IX

Pius IX received both requests with joy. At the very beginning of his pontificate (December 10, 1847), he had set aside the third Sunday after Easter for the feast and the liturgy of the Patronage of St. Joseph. Already in 1854, in a sparkling and fervent talk he had pointed to St. Joseph as the surest hope of the Church after the Blessed Virgin; and on December 8, 1870, when the Vatican Council had been suspended because of political events, he chose the happy coincidence of the feast of the Immaculate Conception for the official proclamation of St. Joseph as Patron of the Universal Church and for the elevation of the feast of March 19 in its liturgical celebration as a double rite of the first class. That decree of December 8, 1870, issued "To the City and to the World," was brief but precious and admirable, truly worthy of the "For Perpetual Memory" since it opened for the successors of Pius IX a mine of the richest and most precious inspiration.

Leo XIII

For the feast of the Assumption in 1889, the immortal Leo XIII issued the letter "Quamquam Pluries", the fullest and richest document which a pope ever issued in honor of the putative father of Jesus, pointing up his characteristic role as the model for fathers of families and for workers. From it originates the beautiful prayer, "To thee, O blessed Joseph," which did so much to fill Our childhood with sweetness.

St. Pius X

The holy Pontiff Pius X added many new expressions of devotion and love for St. Joseph to those of Pope Leo, and he willingly accepted the dedication made to him of a treatice illustrating the devotion (Epist ad R. P. A. Lepicier, O.S.M., February 12, 1908; Acta Pii X, P.M., Rome, 1914, 168–169). He also added to the treasure of indulgences for the recitation of the Litany that is so dear and so pleasing to recite. How expressive are the words used by him in this grant! "Our Most Holy Father Pope Pius X is devoted to the renowned patriarch St. Joseph with a special and constant religious love for him who is the putative father of the Divine Redeemer, the chaste husband of the Virgin Mother of God, and the all powerful Patron before God of the Catholic Church" — and note the depth of personal feeling — "and whose glorious name he received at birth". Note the other words for the announcement of the reasons for these new grants: "In order to increase the veneration of St. Joseph, Patron of the Universal Church".

BENEDICT XV

At the outbreak of the first great European War, when the eyes of St. Pius X had closed on life here below, Pope Benedict XV was providentially raised up to move across the sorrowful years 1914 to 1918 like a kindly star bringing universal consolation. He, too, was quick to promote devotion to the Holy Patriarch. It is to him that we owe the introduction of the two prefaces into the Canon of the mass: that of St. Joseph and that for masses for the dead, happily associating them by issuing the two decrees on the same day, April 9, 1919, as if to remind men of the way in which sorrows and consolation are mingled and shared in the two families: the heavenly family of Nazareth, of which St. Joseph was the legal head, and the immense human family afflicted with universal grief because of the countless victims of the devastating war. What a sorrowful but at the same time consoling and fitting combination: St. Joseph on the one hand, and on the other, St. Michael the standard-bearer, each presenting to the Lord the souls of the departed "into the holy light."

In the following year — July 25, 1920 — Pope Benedict returned to the subject while preparations were being made for the fiftieth anniversary of Pius IX's proclamation of St. Joseph as Patron of the Universal Church. He came back to it in the light of theological doctrines with his "Motu Proprio, *Bonum Sane*", which throughout breathed forth an air of tenderness and unwavering trust. Oh! How beautiful to cast new light on the meek and kindly figure of the Saint, and to have the Christian people call upon him to protect the Church Militant, at the very moment when they were beginning to re-educate their finest efforts to spiritual and material reconstruction in the wake of so many calamities; and finally, to offer consolation to so many millions of human victims, poised on the threshold of their last agony. For these victims, Pope Benedict wished the bishops and many pious societies throughout the world to offer up their prayers to St. Joseph, patron of the dying.

Pius XI and Pius XII

The last two Pontiffs — Pius XI and Pius XII — of dear and venerated memory — showed deep and edifying fidelity to following the same path of recommending fervent devotion to the Holy Patriarch in all of their appeals, their exhortations, and their inspiring words. At least on four different occasions, Pius XI, in solemn allocutions dealing with new saints and very often at the annual celebrations of March 19th, for example in 1928, and again in 1935 and in 1937 took the occasion to exalt St. Joseph: the many glories that shone forth from the spiritual image of the guardian of Jesus, of the chaste husband of Mary, of the pious and modest workman of Nazareth, and of the Patron of the Universal Church, our powerful shield of defense against the efforts of world atheism, intent on wiping out Christian nations.

Pius XII picked up this keynote from his predecessor and made it echo forth in the same tones, in so many allocutions that were always beautiful, sparkling and felicitous. Thus on April 10, 1940, he invited the newlyweds to place themselves under the secure and sweet cloak of the spouse of Mary and in 1945 he called upon the members of Christian associations for working men to honor St. Joseph as their lofty model and as the invincible guardian of their ranks; and ten years later, in 1955, he announced the institution of the annual feast of St. Joseph the Worker. This recently established feast, celebrated on May 1, takes the place of that on the Wednesday of the second week after Easter, while the traditional feast of March 19 will henceforth mark the date of the solemn and definitive celebration of the patronage of St. Joseph over the Universal Church.

This same Holy Father Pius XII was pleased to adorn the heart of St. Joseph with a special garland in the form of a warm prayer recommended to the devotion of priests and faithful throughout the world; he enriched it with many indulgences. It is a prayer of eminently professional and social nature, and therefore well suited for those who find themselves subject to the law of work, which is for them "a law of honor, of a peaceful and holy life, and a prelude to eternal happiness." Among other ideas, it says, "Be with us, O St. Joseph, in our moment of success, when everything beckons us to taste the honest fruits of our fatigue; but most of all be with us and sustain us in the hours of sadness when heaven seems to be closed against us and the very instruments of our labor are about to rebel in our hands".

MARCH 19: DEFINITIVE DATE FOR THE FEAST OF THE PATRONAGE

Venerable Brethren and beloved sons! We felt that it was opportune for Us to propose these notes on history and religious piety for the fervent attention of you souls, trained to a fine sense of how a Christian and

Catholic should live, precisely on this date of March 19, when the feast of St. Joseph coincides with the beginning of Passiontide and prepares us for a deep familiarity with the most impressive and saving mysteries of the sacred Liturgy. The dispositions that lead us to veil the images of Jesus crucified, of Mary, and of the saints during the two weeks which come before Easter, are an invitation to a holy inner recollection concerning our relationships with our Lord in our prayer; it should be a meditation and a supplication that is frequent and ardent. Our Lord, the Blessed Virgin, and the saints are waiting for us to express our trusting, heartfelt prayers; and it is only natural for these prayers to center on things that most closely correspond to the needs of the Catholic Church Universal.

EXPECTATIONS FOR THE ECUMENICAL COUNCIL

There can be no doubt that the Ecumenical Council of the Vatican stands at the center and in first place among these needs and cares; it is now eagerly awaited by all those who believe in Jesus, the Redeemer, and who belong to our Mother, the Catholic Church, or to one of the various groups that are separated from it and yet still anxious — at least as far as many are concerned — for a return to peace and unity that will be in full accord with Christ's teaching and His prayer to His heavenly Father. It is only natural for Us to have as Our aim, in thus recalling the words of the popes of the last century, to stir up the Catholic world to work for the success of this great plan for order, for spiritual improvement and for peace, which constitute the purpose and goal of an Ecumenical Council.

THE COUNCIL AT THE SERVICE OF ALL SOULS

Everything about the Church as Jesus established

it is great and worthy of attention. The celebration of a Council gathers the most distinguished persons of the ecclesiastical world around the fathers: those who are most richly endowed with the gifts of theological and juridical learning, of organizing ability, of apostolic zeal and fervor. This is what a council is: the Pope at the summit, and around him and with him cardinals, bishops from every rite and every country, the best qualified scholars and teachers from various levels and from various fields in which they specialize. But the Council is meant for all Christian people; they have an interest in it, for they will share in the more perfect communication of grace and of Christian vitality that will make it easier for them to acquire more quickly the truly precious goods of the present life and thus assure themselves of the riches of the eternal ages.

All, then, are interested in the Council, clergy and laity, great and small of every part of the world, of every class, of every race, of every color; and if there is a protector to be appointed to obtain from heaven, in its preparation and development, that "divine power" by which it seems destined to mark an epoch in the modern history of the Church, it could not be entrusted to a better heavenly protector than St. Joseph, the august head of the family of Nazareth and protector of Holy Church.

Whenever we listen to the echoes of the voices of the popes of this last century of our history, as We just have done, Our heart is particularly moved by the words of Pius XI, which were so typical of him in their calm and carefully thoughtout way of expression. We recall hearing a discourse pronounced precisely on March 19, 1928, with an allocution which he just would not and could not restrain, in honor of St. Joseph — of the dear and blessed St. Joseph, as he liked to call him.

"It is very thought provoking," he said, "to see two magnificent figures who were close to each other in the beginnings of the Church now standing alongside each other in brilliance: first, that of St. John the Baptist, who rises out of the desert, sometimes with a thundering voice and sometimes with meekness and gentleness; sometimes like a roaring lion and at others like a friend rejoicing in the glory of the bridegroom and offering the wonderful testimony of his martyrdom to the whole world. Then the figure of Peter, so full of vigor, who hears those magnificent words from the Divine Master: "Go, and preach to the whole world"; and to himself personally, "Thou art Peter, and upon this rock I will build My Church." This was a great mission, with divine magnificence and acclaim.

This was what Pius XI had to say; then he continued, so felicitously: "Between these great personages, between these two missions, there appears the mission and the person of St. Joseph, withdrawn, silent, almost unperceived and unknown in humility, in silence which was to shine forth only centuries later, a silence which was to be followed by a resounding chant of glory in the centuries".

Oh! the invocation of St. Joseph! Oh! devotion to St. Joseph for the protection of the Second Ecumenical Council of the Vatican!

Venerable brethren and sons of Rome, brethren and well beloved children of the entire world! This is what We wanted to lead up to and this is why We are sending this apostolic letter on March 19th. We wanted the celebration of the feast of St. Joseph, the Patron of the Universal Church, to bring your souls the inspiration for an extraordinary renewal of fervor that will come from a more lively, more ardent, and more constant prayerful participation in the cares of Holy Church, your teacher and mother, your instructor and guide for this extraordinary event — the Twenty-first Ecumenical Council and the Second of the Vatican — to which the public press of the whole world has been devoting lively interest and respectful attention.

You know very well that the first phase of organizing the Council is moving along calmly, effectively, and in encouraging fashion. Distinguished prelates and clergymen by the hundreds have come from every part of the world and are now meeting here in the City; they have been divided up into various well organized sections, each with responsibility for some important work all its own. They are following the lines laid down by the priceless contents of a series of imposing volumes that have gathered together the thoughts and experience and suggestions that are the fruit of the wisdom, intelligence and apostolic zeal that constitutes the real wealth and treasure of the Catholic Church of the past, the present and the future. All the Ecumenical Council needs in order to reach a successful conclusion is the light of truth and of grace, the discipline of study and of silence, and a serene peace and trust in minds and hearts. This is on the human side. On the other hand, the Christian people must call down God's aid from on high through their prayers and through their efforts to lead model lives that will be a foretaste and a first evidence of the firm determination that each one of the faithful must make to apply and put into practice the teaching and directives that will be proclaimed at the end of the eagerly awaited event — which is now well on its way to what promises to be a successful conclusion.

VENERABLE BRETHREN AND BELOVED CHILDREN!

The luminous thought of Pope Pius XI, on March 19, 1928, still lingers with us. Here in Rome the sacrosanct Cathedral of the Lateran is always resplendent in the glory of the Baptist. But in the great basilica of St. Peter's, where precious mementos of the whole of Christianity are venerated, there is also an altar for St. Joseph, and We intend, and propose on this date, March 19, 1961, that the altar of St. Joseph be adorned with new splendor, more handsomely and more solemnly, and that it become a center of attraction and religious piety for individual souls and for large crowds. It is under the heavenly canopy of the Vatican basilica, around the Head of the Church, that the ranks of the members of the Apostolic College will be united from all parts of the globe, even the most distant, for the Ecumenical Council.

O St. Joseph! It is here, in this very place, that you will exercise your office of "Protector of the Universal Church." It has been our desire to present to you, through the voices and documents of Our immediate predecessors of the last century — from Pius IX through Pius XII — a crown of honor, echoing the testimonies of affectionate veneration which are now ascending from every Catholic nation and every missionary region. Be always our protector. May your interior spirit of peace, of silence, of good works, and of prayer, in the service of the Church, animate us always and make us rejoice, in union with your blessed Spouse, our most sweet and Immaculate Mother, in a most strong and sweet love of Jesus, the glorious and immortal King of ages and peoples. Amen.

Given at Rome, at St. Peter's, March 19, 1961, the third year of Our Pontificate. P.P.John XXIII.

Allocution by Pope John XXIII

On the same day that the Apostolic Letter was officially released, Pope John XXIII addressed various religious communities and Catholic lay organizations. In the allocution he cited several of St. Joseph's tributes and the example of St. Joseph. The following are the pertinent excepts:

You can image what tenderness We feel this morning as We greet you beloved children who have come from every corner of Rome, just a few hours after publication of the Apostolic Letter on devotion to St. Joseph. . . .

As you wonderful laymen and outstanding religious try to come closer to the gentle figure of the guardian of Jesus, you find there the best kind of lesson for all of you as a group and the best kind of example for the special tasks entrusted to each and every one of you. He offers a timely reminder and he supplies that sense of balance and of patience, that love of silence and love of sacrifice which brings soundness and solidity to institutions which are devoted to piety, mutual assistance and spiritual and material improvement.

We would like to share a secret with you today, Cardinal Pietro Gasparri, then Secretary of State, was the one who informed Us of Our nomination as Apostolic Visitor in Bulgaria — a dearly beloved country that We recall with a love that remains unchanged — and of the promotion to the episcopal dignity that would accompany it. When We heard mention of the fact that We would be consecrated on the feast of St. Joseph, and in the church of San Carlo al Corso, he asked Us in that very direct and pointed but friendly way he had: "And why in the world on the feast of St. Joseph?" Our reply was a simple one: "Because this is the Saint We think would be the ideal teacher and patron of diplomats of the Holy See." "Oh, so that's it!" said the Cardinal. "I would never have guessed." "Well, you see, Your Eminence, it's this way. Knowing how to obey; knowing how to keep quiet; when need be, speaking with care and reserve; that is a diplomat of the Holy See, and that is St. Joseph. Just picture him setting out for Bethlehem at once out of obedience; carefully looking for some place to stay; and then watching over the cave; eight days after the birth of Jesus, presiding over the Jewish rite which made a newborn child one of the Chosen People. Just picture him receiving with honor the Magi, those splendid ambassadors from the East. Just see him on the roads of Egypt, and then back at Nazareth, always silent and obedient: showing Jesus to people and hiding Him; defending Him and caring for Him. And as for himself, just following along quietly, remaining in the shadow of the mysteries of the Lord, and seeing a little heavenly light thrown upon them every so often by an angel." "I understand, I see," Cardinal Gasparri replied. "You are right. And if you have any difficulty in picking the person to consecrate you, remember that I have already consecrated many representatives of the Holy See."

This year St. Joseph stands on the threshold of the annual celebrations of the Passion and death of the Savior of the world. If you think it over carefully, this is just the place and just the role in which he and his devout imitators belong: never abandoning the Lord Jesus; not losing courage at the apparent success of the enemy of all good, at the momentary eclipse to be noted in so many, many men whom God loves, an eclipse, one might say, of good judgement, of right conscience, of generous activity.

There is an old saying that fits in here very well. If a person wants to save his soul and feel safe in the house of the Father and preserve the precious gifts of nature and of grace that God has bestowed upon him, all he has to do is examine his conscience on the everlasting teaching of the gospel and of the Church; and St. Joseph's life offers a most attractive example of this teaching.

Permit Us once again to call upon the special protection of St. Joseph and to beg him to obtain the graces of heaven and the consolations of earth for all of you present here, your families and your institutes.

Change in the Canon of the Mass

On November 13, 1962 Pope John XXIII included the name of St. Joseph in the "Communicantes" prayer of the Canon of the Mass. In taking this action, John XXIII led to the permanent mention of St. Joseph in the Constitution on the Church officially enacted by Vatican II.

Brother André Update

Br. André's tomb was opened December 1963 according to the cannonization process. A witness at the time wrote that Brother André's hands were spared the discoloration ensuing from the mummification process of the remains. Though the remainder of the body was found to have turned dark brown in drying up over the years, the hands were much the same color they were when Brother André was interred 27 years earlier. The fingernails too apparently had continued to grow for sometime after death since they now appeared very long, somewhat as if Brother André's hands had been reluctant to die and to cease performing deeds of mercy and healing.

A second finding which was forcefully revealing was made by the attending anatomist. The anatomist had just slit open Brother André's cassock both front and back to proceed with the positive identification of the corpse. When the body was totally shorn of its burial clothes, the anatomist was puzzled with a cord he found girding Brother André's waist. As he raised the time worn cord for all to see, none but the uninitiated could be mistaken: The several knots in the cord definitely identified it as a Saint Joseph's cord worn by Brother André even in death and eloquently witnessing to his unerring devotion to the Blessed Patriarch.

A note of explanation is appropriate regarding the Saint Joseph Cord. The devotion to the Cord of Saint Joseph took its rise in Antwerp, Belgium in 1657 due to a miraculous healing effected by the wearing of this precious girdle. An Augustinian Nun was cured after physicians had declared her death to be inevitable. This was related by the Bollandists and published in 1810. The Cord of St. Joseph was worn, not merely for bodily ailments but also as a preservative of the virtue of purity. On September 19, 1859, the new formula of blessing and permission for its solemn and private use was approved by the Sacred Congregation.

The Cord should be of cotton, wool or linen, ending at one extremity in seven knots, indicative of the joyous, sorrowful and glorious mysteries of the august Patriarch. It is worn as a girdle and ought to be blessed by a priest possessing powers to engird one with it. It should be noted that while Brother André was alive, he was responsible for making the Cords of St. Joseph for the community. While doing so, he fashioned the end threads into a tassel of his own design.

The interior of the basilica at Mount Royal, Montreal was completed in 1966.

First International Symposium

In celebration of the Centennial of the proclamation of St. Joseph as Patron of the Universal Church the First International Symposium on St. Joseph was held in Rome from November 29 to December 6, 1970 at Domus Mariae. 40 Researchers from 9 countries met to analyze the exact meaning of the ancient texts and above all, to show how little by little, the idea of the exceptional mission of the Spouse of Mary in the history of salvation developed. The first efforts were devoted to the figure of St. Joseph in the Bible, then the apocryphal literature of the New Testament, and finally in the writings of the Fathers of the Church. A major part of the studies also concerned the diverse documents from the long period of the Middle Ages: commentaries on Holy Scripture, preaching, theological treatices, literature, liturgy, archeology and iconography (how St. Joseph was pictured in art).

This Symposium traced the origins of theology and of the cult of St. Joseph during the first 15 centuries of the Church.

Brother André's Heart

Brother André's heart was excised at the time of death as a sign of respect. Eventually it was placed on display for veneration by the pilgrims. This was done as a sign of great things to come. In March, 1973, the heart was stolen and held for ransom. On December 21, 1974, the heart was anonymously returned, to the pleasure of the faithful.

Second International Symposium

During September 19 to 26, 1976 the Second International Symposium on St. Joseph was held in Toledo, Spain. Their main goal was to continue the studies into the 16th century. 43 researchers from 11 different countries convened to bring to light the development of devotion to St. Joseph, who was being honored by the multiplication of confraternities, altars, chapels, churches, towns, cities and diocese being named for him.

Br. André, Venerable

On June 12, 1978 Pope Paul VI declared Brother André Venerable, the first step on the way to Canonization.

Third International Symposium

From September 14 to 21, 1980 was held the meeting of the Third International Symposium on St. Joseph. St. Joseph's Oratory was the host, an important event since the Oratory has been hailed as "the world's capital of devotion to St. Joseph." The Symposium celebrated the 75th anniversary of the foundation of St. Joseph's Oratory. The main discussions spoke of how St. Joseph was presented during the 17th Century: in the commentaries on Scripture and theology, in the religious literature and preaching and especially in the liturgy and popular devotion.

Maurice Cardinal Roy, archbishop of Quebec City and Primate of the Canadian Church, who presided over the opening ceremonies touched on the right chord during his homily. He said "St. Joseph's life is a discourse on God. God's Son is God's Word. Joseph hearkens to the Word, he puts it into practice, he dedicates it and takes it for his guideline." In addition to discussion on "Devotion to the Holy Family in New France in the XVIIth Century," His Eminence Paul-Emile Cardinal Leger called attention to three different aspects of St. Joseph's role in the Church: his function as an intercessor, a task contiguous to the dispensation of grace; his vocation as Patron of the Universal Church which has been confirmed gradually over the centuries; and his function as a model to be followed in our relationship to God.

Br. André, Blessed

Br. André was beatified on May 23, 1982 by Pope John Paul II before a crowd of 30,000 pilgrims and visitors gathered on St. Peter's Square at the Vatican. On June 20 a public celebration in Montreal honored the humble client of St. Joseph, now designated as Blessed André.

On September 21, 1982 a resolution was presented in Montreal that Beaver Hall Square should become Place Frere André.

Fourth International Symposium

The Fourth International Symposium of Josephology was held September 22 to 29, 1985 hosted in Kalisz, the oldest city in Poland. This city was chosen because the Church of Kalisz was dedicated to the Holy Family, and has been recognized as a sanctuary of devotion to St. Joseph since the Middle Ages (the world's oldest sanctuary dedicated to St. Joseph). More than 40 specialists from 11 different countries had prepared a study for the symposium. The main themes concerned how veneration of St. Joseph continued to develop during the 17th century.

Place Frere André is dedicated with a statue of Br. André in Montreal on November 2, 1986. August 12, 1987 marked the gala premier of the motion picture on the life of Br. André, *Frere André*. Also during 1987, the bust of Br. André was brought into the Cathedral of Montreal, "Mary Queen of the World and St. James". Further a statue of Br. André was dedicated at Notre Dame University in South Bend, Indiana.

By fostering devotion to his dear and best friend, St. Joseph, Br. André intercedes for countless miracles.

St. Joseph's Oratory, Montreal, Canada (1987)

Let us turn to this great apostle of St. Joseph when we need special assistance.

Permit us to add a footnote to the difference between a shrine and a church. The founding of most of Christendom's great shrines tend to prove the consistancy of God's providential procedures. The Lord strives, so to speak, to demonstrate the conceit of human wisdom in comparison with His divine strategy. He chooses weak and disproportionate instruments, humble and simple souls to convey His message. "Men are capable of building churches, within which they call down God to dwell; but God alone can create shrines and endow them with the secret power of attracting entire populations," wrote Msgr. Freppel.

Because of Br. André's love and devotion to our Lord through St. Joseph, St. Joseph's Oratory was constructed and is the largest shrine in the world dedicated to St. Joseph. St. Joseph's Oratory entices people the world over to return to it again and again and perpetually remains a subject of wonderment for pilgrims. On certain occasions one witnesses titanic human tides surging up the mountainside. Naturally, among these countless pilgrims, are a substantial number of invalids and handicapped of all types, because true shrines have always been considered as havens for suffering humanity. All the miseries and the sorrows rise like mighty waves beating against the promontory upon which St. Joseph has elected to dwell.

CHAPTER TWELVE

After 20 centuries of dissertations on St. Joseph, we are asked to take up devotion to the Holy Patriarch. As many theologians have said, St. Joseph is the patron of all causes and a perfect example of all virtues. Virtues are many, however, as has been said repeatedly, St. Joseph is the perfect model for "all". To enumerate would only leave room for omission. The key is *all*.

Since the Church has deemed to declare St. Joseph Patron of the Universal Church, we, as its children, should do likewise. Fr. Faber said in the mid 19th century that Fr. Gerson was the doctor and theologian for devotion to St. Joseph, St. Teresa was its saint and St. Francis de Sales was its popular leader and missioner. As St. Teresa was in her day, Br. André has become for the 20th century, the instrument of the Lord to make St. Joseph better known and honored.

The day has come for St. Joseph's cultus to be brought to the foreground. Centuries of growth, though ever so slowly, have led us to our current period of history. Bishop Bourget dreamed of having the whole world honor St. Joseph in a church of his own. He could not accomplish his dream. A simple brother, Br. André, was chosen by God to bring St. Joseph to the people of the world. As the children at Fatima said, "Peace would have been delivered to the world by St. Joseph's intercession, had the children not been arrested." If we learn to live according to the will of God, St. Joseph will intercede to bring peace to the world. St. Joseph desires to free us from our afflictions, if only we will be more diligent in our faith. As Br. André said: "You must go to confession, then to communion, then ask St. Joseph your favor."

As we discover St. Joseph we must look to Jesus

in whom we find the hidden life of Joseph. It would appear that much information was left unsaid, yet Scripture is flawless, telling us no more, nor less than we need to know. As little as is said, even more seems to be said of Joseph. The Gospels tell us that St. Joseph was placed in the position of Head of the Holy Family. Even so, he remained in the background watching, guarding and protecting his Spouse and the child Jesus. The theologians have expounded on his virtues. The popes have given their acclaim, asking the faithful to take up devotion to St. Joseph. The author says the same: *Ité ad Joseph, Go to Joseph.*

Let the entire Christian community hold this dear saint near to their heart. If they do so they are able to be even closer to Jesus and Mary, thus they keep the Holy Family as the unit that God intended. If Jesus and Mary obeyed Joseph while on earth, as the theologians have proposed, would they not also obey and grant St. Joseph's wishes in Heaven. Let us keep St. Joseph as our model so that our families may also be one unit. As a mission priest once said: "If a mother and her children attend mass, they are people residing in the same household who attend mass together. However, if the father joins them, they are now a Christian family attending mass. In our day when there are so many single parent families, St. Joseph can give us the strength to cope, just as he did for the Holy Family in Nazareth. Where there is no father, ask St. Joseph to be the father of the household. He will be there.

Today we should reflect on the life of St. Joseph and remember to ask him for his intercession. St. Joseph is renowned for aiding all those who have great devotion to him. Individual examples would be too numerous to mention, however, the life of Br. André and his continuing work gives us a perfect model. If we turn to Br. André as our guide with complete confidence in St. Joseph, we will gain a true friend and confidant. Br. André is a contemporary model showing extraordinary confidence in the love St. Joseph has for us. We know there is nothing that St. Joseph will not give us if we only ask. For those struggling with the trials of everyday life, pray as Br. André taught:

"O good St. Joseph, grant me what you yourself would ask if you were in my place on earth, with a family, and numerous financial difficulties to overcome. Good St. Joseph of Mount Royal, be my help, hear my prayer. Amen."

There is so much to learn from St. Joseph if we would only ask him to teach us. He is waiting for the invitation. You will find that he directs us to his beloved Spouse and our Savior, Jesus Christ. Don't delay, the rewards are great.

We recently completed a Marian Year. This is good for the faithful, but more important would be a year for the Holy Family, dedicated to stressing the importance of the family. We need to stress respect for our spouses as well as the true nurturing of our children. As members of the Christian community we know we need vocations. Yet, as parents, we are more concerned with a love for the world: a good job, a nice home, how successful our children will be, will we have grandchildren. There seems to be a fear that when someone is called to a religious vocation, they are a failure and I would guess by the world's standards, maybe they are. But in God's eye they are saying *yes* to His invitation to do His Will.

Let us rethink what it is to have the call to a religious life. Whether it be as an adult, or as children, isn't that the greatest gift God can give. Why do we react like it is a curse. We pray for vocations, only to say silently to ourselves, as long as God does not choose from my family. Some years ago when worldly opportunities were not so great, our loved ones were encouraged to vocations. Why should it be different today? Everyone is called to encourage each other to answer the call as Mary and Joseph did and say "yes" to whatever God wills. We need only take the time to listen and then respond with a joyous YES.

We hope for pleasant family relations whether it be our personal, parish or community family. But we face disappointment if we do not include the greatest family that ever lived in any of those relations. They must be part of our daily lives, not just on the feast of the Holy Family. If we want harmony in our homes, parishes and communities, which can lead to "peace in the world", we need the strength of the Holy Family under the guidance and protection of St. Joseph.

This concept has been around for centuries, although not always taught as a precept of our faith. Salvation, naturally, comes from our Lord, Jesus Christ, but when we join Mary and Joseph to Jesus, then nothing is impossible. They will intercede to God, so that whatever we need, our prayers will be answered.

Our family structure has faltered over the last few years. If we have confidence in Jesus, Mary and Joseph, that family unit can again be strong and secure.

"Ité ad Joseph." By doing so you must go to Mary and you will know our Lord. There is nothing greater. The three are inseparable as they lived on earth one for the other.

The following was given to us as "the" explanation of a tapestry, written by Catherine Lower O'Shea. Simply put, it explains "The Tapestry of St. Joseph," still unfinished.

A young monk once spent months at a Belgium monastery helping to weave a tapestry. One day, he rose from his bench in disgust: "I can't do this any longer!" he exclaimed. "My directions make no sense. I have been working with a bright yellow thread, and suddenly I'm to knot and cut it short, for no reason. What a waste."

"My son," said an older monk, "you are not seeing this tapestry correctly. You are sitting at the back, working on only one spot."

He led the young man to the front of the tapestry, hanging stretched in the huge workroom, and the novice gasped. He had been weaving a beautiful picture, the three Kings paying homage to the Christ Child. His yellow thread was part of the gleaming halo around the baby's head. What had seemed wasteful and senseless was magnificent.

We are all part of a larger pattern, the full beauty of which we may never see.

As times goes on many more threads will be added to the tapestry which, with God's intervention will reveal to the world the beauty and importance of Saint Joseph and his part in the Divine Plan.

Epilogue

1989 has been beneficial to the cultus of St. Joseph. Since the manuscript was completed two events have taken place which deserve mention.

The first is an Apostolic Letter by Pope John Paul II, delivered on August 15th. "Redemptoris Custos" was given on the Solemnity of the Assumption of the Blessed Virgin celebrating the centenary of the encyclical "Quamquam Pluries." The original translation was published in the Vatican newspaper "L'Observatore Romano" (October 30, 1989). The following is the complete translation of this wonderful document.

Redemptoris Custos

To Bishops
To Priests and Deacons
To Men and Women Religious
And to all the Lay Faithful

Introduction

1. Called to be the Guardian of the Redeemer, *"Joseph did as the angel of the Lord commanded him and took his wife"* (cf. Mt 1:24).

Inspired by the Gospel, the Fathers of the Church from the earliest centuries stressed that just as Saint Joseph took loving care of Mary and gladly dedicated himself to Jesus Christ's upbringing, he likewise watches over and protects Christ's Mystical Body, that is, the Church, of which the Virgin Mary is the exemplar and model.

On the occasion of the centenary of Pope Leo XIII's Encyclical Epistle *Quamquam Pluries,* and in line with the veneration given to Saint Joseph over the centuries, I wish to offer for your consideration, dear brothers and sisters, some reflections concerning him "to whose custody God entrusted his most precious treasures." I gladly fulfill this pastoral duty so that all may grow in devotion to the Patron of the Universal Church and in love for the Saviour whom he served in such an exemplary manner.

In this way the whole Christian people not only will turn to Saint Joseph with greater fervor and invoke his patronage with trust, but also always keep before their eyes his humble, mature way of serving and of "taking part" in the plan of salvation.

I am convinced that by reflection upon the way that Mary's spouse shared in the divine mystery, the Church — on the road towards the future with all of humanity — will be enabled to discover ever anew her own identity within this redemptive plan, *which is founded on the mystery of the Incarnation.*

This is precisely the mystery in which Joseph of Nazareth "shared" like no other human being except Mary, the Mother of the Incarnate Word. He shared in it with her; he was involved in the same salvific event; he was the guardian of the same love, through the power of which the eternal Father "destined us to be his sons through Jesus Christ" (Eph 1:5).

I The Gospel portrait

Marriage to Mary

2. "Joseph, Son of David, *do not fear to take Mary* your wife, for that which is conceived in her is of the Holy Spirit; she will bear a son, and you shall call his name Jesus, for he will save his people from their sins" (Mt 1:20–21).

In these words we find the core of biblical truth about Saint Joseph; they refer to that moment in his life to which the Fathers of the Church make special reference.

The Evangelist Matthew explains the significance of this moment while also describing how Joseph lived it. However, in order to understand fully both its content and context, it is important to keep in mind the parallel passage in the *Gospel of Luke.* In Matthew we read: "Now the birth of Jesus Christ took place in this way. When his mother Mary had been betrothed to Joseph, before they came together she was found to be with child of the Holy Spirit" (Mt 1:18). However, the origin of Mary's pregnancy "of the Holy Spirit" is described more fully and explicitly in *what Luke tells us about the Annunciation of Jesus' birth:* "The angel Gabriel was sent from God to a city of Galilee named Nazareth, to a virgin betrothed to a man whose name was Joseph, of the house of David; and the virgin's name was Mary" (Lk 1:26–27). The angel's greeting, "Hail, full of grace, the Lord is with you" (Lk 1:28) created an inner turmoil in Mary and also moved her to reflect. Then the messenger reassured the Virgin and at the same time revealed God's special plan for her: "*Do not be afraid, Mary, for you have found favor with God. And behold, you will conceive in your womb and bear a son,* and you shall call his name Jesus. He will be great, and be called the Son of the Most High; and the Lord God will give to him the throne of his father David" (Lk 1:30–32).

A little earlier the Gospel writer had stated that at the moment of the Annunciation, Mary was "betrothed to a man whose name was Joseph, of the house of David." The nature of this *marriage* is explained indirectly when Mary, after hearing what the messenger says about the birth of the child, asks, "How can this be, *since I do not know man?*" (Lk 1:34). The angel responds: "The Holy Spirit will come upon you, and the power of the Most High will overshadow you; therefore the child to be born will be called holy, the Son of God" (Lk 1:35). Although Mary is already "wedded" to Joseph, she will remain a virgin, because the child conceived in her at the Annunciation was conceived by the power of the Holy Spirit.

At this point Luke's text coincides with Matthew 1:18 and serves to explain what we read there. If, after her marriage to Joseph, Mary "is found to be with child of the Holy Spirit," this fact corresponds to all that the Annunciation means, in particular to Mary's final words: *"Let it be to me according to your word"* (Lk 1:38). In response to what is clearly the plan of God, with the passing of days and weeks Mary's "pregnancy" is visible to the people and to Joseph; she appears before them as one who must give birth and carry within herself the mystery of motherhood.

3. In these circumstances, "her husband Joseph, being a just man and unwilling to put her to shame, *resolved to send her away quietly"* (Mt 1:19). He did not know how to deal with Mary's "astonishing" motherhood. He certainly sought an answer to this unsettling question, but above all he sought a way out of what was for him a difficult situation. *"But as he considered this,* behold, an angel of the Lord appeared to him in a dream, saying, '*Joseph,* son of David, *do not fear to take Mary your wife,* for that which is conceived in her is of the Holy Spirit; she will bear a son, and you shall call his name Jesus, for he will save his people from their sins'" (Mt 1:20–21).

There is a strict parallel between the "annunciation" in Matthew's text and the one in Luke. *The divine messenger introduces Joseph to the mystery of Mary's motherhood.* While remaining a virgin, she who by law is his "spouse" has become a mother through the power of the Holy Spirit. And when the Son in Mary's womb comes into the world, he must receive the name Jesus. This was a name known among the Israelites and sometimes given to their sons. In this case, however, *it is the Son who,* in accordance with the divine promise, *will bring to perfect fulfillment the meaning of the name Jesus* — 'Yehosua' which means *God saves.*

Joseph is visited by *the messenger* as Mary's spouse," as the one who in due time must give this name to the Son to be born of the Virgin of Nazareth who is married to him. It is *to Joseph,* then that the messenger turns, *entrusting to him the responsibilities of an earthly father with regard to Mary's Son.*

"When Joseph woke from sleep, he did as the angel of the Lord commanded him and took Mary as his wife" (cf. Mt 1:24). He took her in all the mystery of her motherhood. He took her together with the Son who had come into the world by the power of the Holy Spirit. In this way *he showed a readiness of will like Mary's* with regard to what God asked of him through the angel.

II The guardian of the Mystery of God

4. When, soon after the Annunciation, Mary went to the house of Zechariah to visit her kinswoman Elizabeth, even as she offered her greeting she heard the words of Elizabeth, who was "filled with the Holy Spirit" (Lk 1:41). Besides offering a salutation which recalled that of the angel at the Annunciation, Elizabeth also said: *"and blessed is she who believed that there would be a fulfillment of what was spoken to her from the Lord"* (Lk 1:45). These words were the guiding thought of the Encyclical, *Redemptoris Mater* in which I sought to deepen the teaching of the Second Vatican Council, which stated: *"The Blessed Virgin advanced in her pilgrimage of faith,* and faithfully preserved her union with her Son even to the Cross," "preceding" all those who follow Christ by faith.

Now at the beginning of this pilgrimage, *the faith of Mary meets the faith of Joseph.* If Elizabeth said of the Redeemer's Mother, "blessed is she who believed," in a certain sense this blessedness can be referred to Joseph as well, since he responded positively to the word of God when it was communicated to him at the decisive moment. While it is true that Joseph did not respond to the angel's "announcement" in the same way as Mary, he "*did* as the angel of the Lord commanded him and took his wife." *What he did is the clearest "obedience of faith"* (cf. Rom 1:5; 16:26; 2 Cor 10:5–6).

One can say that *what Joseph did* united him in an altogether special way to the faith of Mary. *He accepted* as a truth coming from God *the very thing that she had already accepted* at the Annunciation. The Council teaches: "'The obedience of faith' must be given to God as he reveals himself. By this obedience of faith man freely commits himself entirely to God, making 'the full submission of his intellect and will to God who reveals,' and willingly assenting to the revelation given by him." *This statement,* which touches the very essence of faith, *is perfectly applicable to Joseph of Nazareth.*

5. Therefore he became *a unique guardian of the mystery* "hidden for ages in God" (Eph 3:9), as did Mary, in that decisive moment which Saint Paul calls *"the fullness of time,"* when "God sent forth his Son, born of woman... to redeem those who were under the law, so that we might receive adoption as sons" (Gal 4:4–5). In the words of the council: "It pleased God, in his goodness and wisdom, to reveal himself and to make known the mystery of his will (cf. Eph 1:9). His will was that men should have access to the Father, through Christ, the Word made flesh, in the Holy Spirit, and became sharers in the divine nature (cf. Eph 2:18; 2Pt 1:4)."

Together with Mary, Joseph is the first guardian of this divine mystery. Together with Mary, and in relation to Mary, *he shares in this final phase of God's self revelation in Christ,* and he does so from the very beginning. Looking at the Gospel texts of both Matthew and Luke, one can also say that Joseph is the first *to share in the faith of the Mother of God,* and that in doing so he supports his spouse in the faith of the divine Annunciation. He is also the first to be placed by God on the path of Mary's "pilgrimage of faith." It is a path along which — especially at the time of Calvary and Pentecost — Mary will precede in a perfect way.

6. The path that was Joseph's — *his pilgrimage of faith — ended first,* that is to say, before Mary stood at the foot of the Cross on Golgotha, and before that time after Christ returned to the Father, when she was present in the Upper Room on Pentecost, the day the Church was manifested to the world, having been born in the power of the Spirit of truth. Nevertheless, *Joseph's way of faith moved in the same direction:* it was totally determined by the same mystery, of which he, together with Mary, had been the first guardian. The Incarnation and Redemption constitute an organic and indissoluble unity, in which "the plan of revelation is realized by words and deeds which are intrinsically bound up with each other." Precisely because of this unity, Pope John XXIII, who had a great devotion to Saint Joseph, directed that Joseph's name be inserted in the Roman Canon of the Mass — which is the perpetual memorial of redemption — after the name of Mary and before the Apostles, Popes and Martyrs.

The service of Fatherhood

7. As can be deduced from the Gospel texts, Joseph's marriage to Mary is the Juridical basis of his fatherhood. It was to assure fatherly protection for

Jesus that God chose Joseph to be Mary's spouse. It follows that Joseph's fatherhood — a relationship that places him as close as possible to Christ, to whom every election and predestination is ordered (cf. Rom 8:28–29) — comes to pass through marriage to Mary, that is, through the family.

While clearly affirming that Jesus was conceived by the power of the Holy Spirit, and that virginity remained intact in the marriage (cf. Mt 1:18–25; Lk 1:26–38), the Evangelists refer to Joseph as Mary's husband and to Mary as his wife (cf. Mt 1:16, 18–20, 24; Lk 1:27; 2:5).

And while it is important for the Church to profess *the virginal conception of Jesus,* it is no less important to uphold *Mary's marriage to Joseph,* because juridically Joseph's fatherhood depends on it. Thus one understands why the generations are listed according to the genealogy of Joseph: "Why," Saint Augustine asks, "should they not be according to Joseph? Was he not Mary's husband?... Scripture states, through the authority of an Angel, that he was her husband. *Do not fear,* says the Angel, *to take Mary your wife, for that which is conceived in her is of the Holy Spirit.* Joseph was told to name the child, although not born from his seed. *She will bear a son,* the Angel says, *and you will call him Jesus. Scripture recognizes that Jesus is not born of Joseph's seed, since in his concern about the origin of Mary's pregnancy, Joseph is told that it is of the Holy Spirit.* Nonetheless, he is not deprived of his fatherly authority from the moment that he is told to name the child. Finally, even the Virgin Mary, well aware that she has not conceived Christ as a result of conjugal relations with Joseph, still calls him *Christ's father.*"

The *Son of Mary* is also *Joseph's Son* by virtue of the marriage bond that unites them: "By reason of their faithful marriage *both of them* deserve to be called Christ's parents, not only his mother, but also his father, who was a parent in the same way that he was the mother's spouse: *in mind,* not in the flesh." In this marriage none of the requisites of marriage were lacking: "In Christ's parents all the goods of marriage were realized — offspring, fidelity, the sacrament: The *offspring* being the Lord Jesus himself; *fidelity,* since there was no adultery: the *sacrament,* since there was no divorce."

Analyzing the nature of marriage, both Saint Augustine and Saint Thomas always identify it with an "indivisible union of souls," a "union of hearts," with "consent." These elements are found in an exemplary manner in the marriage of Mary and Joseph. At the culmination of the history of salvation, when God reveals his love for humanity through the gift of the word, it is precisely *the marriage of Mary and Joseph* that brings to realization in full "freedom" the "spousal gift of self" in receiving and expressing such a love. "In this great undertaking which is the renewal of all things in Christ, marriage — it too purified and renewed — becomes a new reality, a sacrament of the New Covenant. We see that at the beginning of the New Testament, as at the beginning of the Old, there is a married couple. But whereas Adam and Eve were the source of evil which was unleashed on the world, Joseph and Mary are the summit from which holiness spreads all over the earth. The Saviour began the work of salvation by this virginal and holy union, wherein is manifested his all powerful will to *purify and sanctify the family* — that sanctuary of love and cradle of life."

How much the family of today can learn from this! "The essence and role of the family are in the final analysis specified by love. Hence the family has *the mission to guard, reveal and communicate love,* and this is a living reflection of and a real sharing in God's love for humanity and the love of Christ the Lord for the Church his bride." This being the case, it is in the Holy Family, the original "Church in miniature (*Ecclesia domestica*)," that every Christian family must be reflected. "Through God's mysterious design, it was in that family that the Son of God spent long years of a hidden life. It is therefore the prototype and example for all Christian families."

8. Saint Joseph was called by God to serve the person and mission of Jesus directly *through the exercise of his fatherhood.* It is precisely in this way that, as the Church's Liturgy teaches, he "cooperated in the fullness of time in the great mystery of salvation" and is truly a "minister of salvation." His fatherhood is expressed concretely "in his having made his life a service, a sacrifice to the mystery of the incarnation and to the redemptive mission connected with it; in having used the legal authority which was his over the Holy Family in order to make a total gift of self, of his life and work; in having turned his human vocation to domestic love into a superhuman oblation of self, an oblation of his heart and all his abilities into love placed at the service of the Messiah growing up in his house."

In recalling that "the beginnings of our redemption" were entrusted "to the faithful care of Joseph," the Liturgy specifies that "God placed him at the head of his family, as a faithful and prudent servant, so that with fatherly care he might watch over his only-begotten Son." Leo XIII emphasized the sublime nature of this mission: "He among all stands out in his august dignity, since by divine disposition he was guardian, and according to human opinion, father of God's Son. Whence it followed that the Word of God was subjected to Joseph, he obeyed him and rendered to him that honor and reverence that children owe to their father."

Since it is inconceivable that such a sublime task would not be matched by the necessary qualities to adequately fulfill it, we must recognize that Joseph showed Jesus "by a special gift from heaven, all the natural love, all the affectionate solicitude that a father's heart can know."

Besides fatherly authority over Jesus, God also gave Joseph a share in the corresponding love, the love that has its origin in the Father "from whom every family in heaven and on earth is named" (Eph 3:15).

The Gospels clearly describe the fatherly responsibility of Joseph towards Jesus. For salvation — which comes through the humanity of Jesus — is realized in actions which are an everyday part of family life, in keeping with that "condescension" which is inherent in the economy of the Incarnation. The gospel writers carefully show how in the life of Jesus nothing was left to chance, but how everything took place according to God's predetermined plan. The oft-repeated formula, "This happened so that there might be fulfilled...," in reference to a particular event in the Old Testament, serves to emphasize the unity and continuity of the plan which is fulfilled in Christ.

With the incarnation, the "promises" and "figures" of the Old Testament became "reality": places, persons, events and rites interrelate according to precise divine commands communicated by Angels and received by creatures who are particularly sensitive to the voice of God. Mary is the Lord's humble servant, prepared from eternity for the task of being Mother of God. Joseph is the one whom God chose to be the "overseer of the Lord's birth," the one who has the responsibility to look after the Son of God's "ordained" entry into the world, in accordance with divine dispositions and human laws. All of the so-called "private" or "hidden" life of Jesus is entrusted to Joseph's guardianship.

The census

9. Journeying to Bethlehem for the census in obedience to the orders of legitimate authority, Joseph fulfilled for the child the significant task of officially inserting the name "Jesus, son of Joseph of Nazareth" (cf. Jn 1:45) in the registry of the Roman Empire. This registration clearly shows that Jesus belongs to the human race as a man among men, a citizen of this world, subject to laws and civil institutions, but also *"saviour of the world."* Origen gives a good description of the theological significance, by no means marginal, of this historical fact: "Since the first census of the whole world took place under Caesar Augustus, and among all the others Joseph too went to register together with Mary his wife, who was with child, and since Jesus was born before the census was completed: to the person who makes a careful examination it will appear that a kind of mystery is expressed in the fact that at the time when all people in the world presented themselves to be counted, Christ too should be counted. By being registered with everyone, he could sanctify everyone; inscribed with the whole world in the census, he offered to the world communion with himself, and after presenting himself he wrote all the people of the world in the book of the living, so that as many as believed in him could then be written in heaven with the saints of God, to whom be glory and power for ever and ever. Amen."

The birth at Bethlehem

10. As guardian of the mystery "hidden for ages in the mind of God," which begins to unfold before his eyes "in the fullness of time," *Joseph, together with Mary,* is a privileged witness to the birth of the Son of God into the world *on Christmas night in Bethlehem.* Luke writes: *"And while they were there, the time came for her to be delivered. And she gave*

birth to her first-born son and wrapped him in swaddling cloths, and laid him in a manger, because there was no place for them in the inn" (Lk 2:6–7).

Joseph was an eyewitness to this birth, which took place in conditions that, humanly speaking, were embarrassing — a first announcement of that "self-emptying" (cf. Phil 2:5–8) which Christ freely accepted for the forgiveness of sins. Joseph also *witnessed the adoration of the shepherds* who arrived at Jesus' birthplace after the angel had brought them the great and happy news (cf. Lk 2:15–16). Later he also *witnessed the homage of the Magi who came from the East* (cf. Mt 2:11).

The Circumcision

11. A son's circumcision was the first religious obligation of a father, and with this ceremony (cf. Lk 2:21) Joseph exercised his right and duty with regard to Jesus.

The principle which holds that all the rites of the Old Testament are a shadow of the reality (cf. Heb 9:9f; 10:1) serves to explain why Jesus would accept them. As with all the other rites, circumcision too is "fulfilled" in Jesus. God's covenant with Abraham, of which circumcision was the sign (cf. Gen 17:13), reaches its full effect and perfect realization in Jesus, who is the "yes" of all the ancient promises (cf. 2 Cor 1:20).

Conferral of the name

12. At the circumcision Joseph names the child "Jesus." This is the only name in which there is salvation (cf. Acts 4:12). Its significance had been revealed to Joseph at the moment of his "annunciation": "You shall call the child Jesus, for he will save his people from their sins" (cf. Mt 1:21). In conferring the name, Joseph declares his own legal fatherhood over Jesus, and in speaking the name he proclaims the child's mission as Saviour.

The Presentation of Jesus in the Temple

13. This rite, to which Luke refers (2:22ff.), includes the ransom of the first-born and sheds light on the subsequent stay of Jesus in the temple at the age of twelve.

The *ransoming of the first-born* is another obligation of the father, and it is fulfilled by Joseph. Represented in the first-born is the people of the covenant, ransomed from slavery in order to belong to God. Here too, Jesus — who is the true "price" of ransom (cf. 1Cor 6:20; 7:23; 1Pt 1:19) — not only "fulfills" the Old Testament rite, but at the same time transcends it, since he is not a subject to be redeemed, but the very author of redemption.

The Gospel writer notes that "his father and his mother marvelled at what was said about him" (Lk 2:23), in particular at *what Simeon said* in his canticle to God, when he referred to Jesus as the "salvation which you have prepared in the presence of all peoples, a light for revelation to the Gentiles, and for glory to your people Israel" and as a "sign that is spoken against" (cf. Lk 2:30–34).

The flight into Egypt

14. After the presentation in the Temple the Evangelist Luke notes: "And when they had performed everything according to the law of the Lord, *They returned into Galilee,* to their own city, Nazareth. And the child grew and became strong, filled with wisdom; and the favor of God was upon him" (Lk 2:39–40).

But *according to Matthew's text,* a very important event took place before the return to Galilee, an event in which divine providence once again had recourse to Joseph. We read: "Now when (the Magi) had departed, behold, an angel of the Lord appeared to Joseph in a dream and said, *'Rise, take the child and his mother, and flee to Egypt,* and remain there till I tell you; for Herod is about to search for the child, to destroy him'" (Mt 2:13). Herod learned from the Magi who came from the East about the birth of the "king of the Jews" (Mt 2:2). And when the Magi departed, he "sent and killed all the male children in Bethlehem and in all that region who were two years old or under" (Mt 2:16). By killing them all, he wished to kill the newborn "king of the Jews" whom he had heard about. And so, Joseph, having been warned in a dream, took the child and his mother by night, and *departed to Egypt,* and remained there *until the death of Herod.* This was to fulfill what the Lord had spoken by the prophet, 'Out of Egypt have I called my son'" (Mt 2:14–15; cf. Hos 11:1).

And so Jesus' way back to Nazareth from Bethlehem passed through Egypt. Just as Israel had followed the path of the exodus "from the condition of slavery" in order to begin the Old Covenant, *so Joseph, guardian and cooperator in the providential mystery of God,* even in exile watched over the one who brings about the New Covenant.

Jesus' stay in the Temple

15. From the time of the Annunciation, both Joseph and Mary found themselves, in a certain sense, *at the heart of the mystery* hidden for ages in the mind of God, a mystery which had taken on flesh: *"The Word became flesh and dwelt among us"* (Jn 1:14). He dwelt among men, within the surroundings of *the Holy Family of Nazareth* — one of many families in this small town of Galilee, one of the many families of the land of Israel. There Jesus "grew and became strong, filled with wisdom; and the favor of God was upon him" (Lk 2:40). The Gospels summarize in a few words the *long period of the "hidden" life,* during which Jesus prepared himself for his messianic mission. Only one episode from this "hidden time" is described in the

Gospel of Luke: the Passover in Jerusalem when Jesus was twelve years old.

Together with Mary and Joseph, Jesus took part in the feast as a young pilgrim. "And when the feast was ended, as they were returning, the boy Jesus stayed behind in Jerusalem. His parents did not know it" (Lk 2:43). After a day's journey, they noticed his absence and began to search "among their kinsfolk and acquaintances." "After three days *they found him in the temple,* sitting among the teachers, listening to them and asking them questions; and all who heard him were amazed at his understanding and his answers" (Lk 2:47). Mary asked: "Son, why have you treated us so? *Behold, your father and I have been looking for you anxiously"* (Lk 2:48). The answer Jesus gave was such that "they did not understand the saying which he spoke to them." He had said, "How is it that you sought me? Did you not know *that I must be in my Father's house?"* (Lk 2:49–50).

Joseph, of whom Mary had just used the words "your father," heard this answer. That, after all, is what all the people said and thought: Jesus was "the son (as was supposed) of Joseph" (Lk 3:23). Nonetheless, the reply of Jesus in the Temple brought once again to the mind of his "presumed father" what he had heard on that night twelve years earlier: "Joseph... do not fear to take Mary your wife, for *that which is conceived in her is of the Holy Spirit."* From that time onwards he knew that he was a guardian of the mystery of God, and it was *precisely this mystery* that the twelve-year-old *Jesus brought to mind:* "I must be in my Father's house."

The support and education of Jesus of Nazareth

16. The growth of Jesus " in wisdom and in stature, and in favor with God and man" (Lk 2:52) took place within the Holy Family under the eyes of Joseph, who

had the important task of "raising" Jesus, that is, feeding, clothing and educating him in the Law and in a trade, in keeping with the duties of a father.

In the Eucharistic Sacrifice, the Church venerates the memory of Mary the ever Virgin Mother of God and the memory of Saint Joseph, because "he fed him whom the faithful must eat as the bread of eternal life."

For his part, Jesus "was obedient to them" (Lk 2:51), respectfully returning the affection of his "parents." In this way he wished to sanctify the obligations of the family and of work, which he performed at the side of Joseph.

III A just man — a husband

17. In the course of that pilgrimage of faith which was his life, Joseph, like Mary, remained faithful to God's call until the end. While Mary's life was the bringing to fullness of that *fiat* first spoken at the Annunciation, *at the moment of Joseph's own "annunciation"* he said nothing; instead he simply *"did* as the angel of the Lord commanded him" (Mt 1:24). And *this first "doing" became the beginning of "Joseph's way."* The Gospels do not record any word ever spoken by Joseph along the way. But *the silence of Joseph* has its own special eloquence, for thanks to that silence we can understand the truth of the Gospels judgement that he was "a just man" (Mt 1:19).

One must come to understand this truth, for it contains *one of the most important testimonies concerning man and his vocation.* Through many generations the Church has read this testimony with ever greater attention and with deeper understanding, drawing, as it were, "what is new and what is old" (Mt 13:52) from the storehouse of the noble figure of Joseph.

18. Above all, the "just" man of Nazareth possesses the clear characteristics of a husband. Luke refers to

Mary as "a virgin betrothed to a man whose name was Joseph" (Lk 1:27). Even before the "mystery hidden for ages" (Eph 3:9) began to be fulfilled, the Gospels set before us *the image of husband and wife*. According to Jewish custom, marriage took place in two stages: first, the legal, or true marriage was celebrated, and then, only after a certain period of time, the husband brought the wife into his own house. Thus, before he lived with Mary, Joseph was already her "husband." *Mary, however, preserved her deep desire to give herself exclusively to God.* One may well ask how this desire of Mary's could be reconciled with a "wedding." The answer can only come from the saving events as they unfold, from the special action of God himself. From the moment of the Annunciation, Mary knew that *she was to fulfill her virginal desire* to give herself exclusively and fully to God precisely *by becoming the Mother of God's Son*. Becoming a Mother by the power of the Holy Spirit was the form taken by her gift of self: a form which God himself expected of the Virgin Mary, who was "betrothed" to Joseph. Mary uttered her *fiat*.

The fact that Mary was "betrothed" to Joseph was *part of the very plan of God*. This is pointed out by Luke and especially by Matthew. The words spoken to Joseph are very significant: "Do not fear to take Mary *your wife,* for that which *she* has been conceived in her is of the Holy Spirit" (Mt 1:20). These words explain the mystery of Joseph's wife: in her motherhood Mary is a virgin. In her, "the Son of the Most High" assumed a human body and became "the Son of Man."

Addressing Joseph through the words of the angel, God speaks to him *as the husband of the Virgin of Nazareth*. What took place in her through the power of the Holy Spirit also *confirmed in a special way the marriage bond* which already existed between Joseph and Mary. God's messenger was clear in what he said to Joseph: "Do not fear to take Mary *your wife* into your home." Hence, what had taken place earlier, namely, Joseph's marriage to Mary, happened in accord with God's will and was meant to endure. In her divine motherhood Mary had to continue to live as "a virgin, the wife of her husband" (cf. Lk 1:27).

19. In the words of the "annunciation" by night, Joseph not only heard the divine truth concerning his wife's indescribable vocation; he *also heard once again the truth about his own vocation.* This "just" man, who, in the spirit of the noblest traditions of the Chosen People, loved the virgin of Nazareth and was bound to her by a husband's love, was once again called by God to this love.

"Joseph did as the angel of the Lord commanded him; he took his wife" into his home (Mt 1:24); what was conceived in Mary was "of the Holy Spirit." From expressions such as these are we not to suppose that his *love as a man was also given new birth by the Holy Spirit?* Are we not to think that the love of God which has been poured forth into the human heart through the Holy Spirit (cf. Rom 5:5), molds every human love to perfection? This love of God also molds — in a completely unique way the love of husband and wife, deepening within it everything of human worth and beauty, everything that bespeaks an exclusive gift of self, a covenant between persons, and an authentic communion according to the model of the Blessed Trinity.

"Joseph... took his wife; *but he knew her not,* until she had borne a son" (Mt 1:24–25). These words indicate *another kind of closeness in marriage.* The deep spiritual closeness arising from marital union and the interpersonal contact between man and woman have their definitive origin in the Spirit, the Giver of Life (cf. Jn 6:63). *Joseph, in obedience to the Spirit, found in the Spirit the source of love,* the conjugal love which he experienced as a man. And this love proved to be greater than this "just man" could ever have expected within the limits of his human heart.

20. In the Liturgy, Mary is celebrated as "united to Joseph, the just man, by a bond of marital and virginal love." There are really two kinds of love here, both of which *together* represent the mystery of the Church — virgin and spouse — as symbolized in the marriage of Mary and Joseph. "Virginity or celibacy for the sake of the Kingdom of God not only does not contradict the dignity of marriage but presupposes and confirms it. Marriage and virginity are two ways of expressing and living the one mystery of the Covenant of God with his people," the Covenant which is a communion of love between God and human beings.

Through his complete self-sacrifice, Joseph expressed his generous love for the Mother of God, and gave her a husband's "gift of self." Even though he decided to draw back so as not to interfere in the plan of God which was coming to pass in Mary, Joseph obeyed the explicit command of the angel and took Mary into his home, while respecting the fact that she belonged exclusively to God.

On the other hand, it was from his marriage to Mary that Joseph derived his singular dignity and his rights in regard to Jesus. "It is certain that the dignity of the Mother of God is so exalted that nothing could be more sublime; yet because Mary was united to Joseph by the bond of marriage, there can be no doubt but that *Joseph approached as no other person ever could* that eminent dignity whereby the Mother of God towers above all creatures. Since marriage is the highest degree of association and friendship, involving by its very nature a communion of goods, it follows that

God, by giving Joseph to the Virgin, did not give him to her only as a companion for life, a witness of her virginity and protector of her honor: he also gave Joseph to Mary in order that *he might share,* through the marriage pact, in her own sublime greatness."

21. This *bond of charity was the core of the Holy Family's life,* first in the poverty of Bethlehem, then in their exile in Egypt, and later in the house of Nazareth. The Church deeply venerates this Family, and proposes it as the model of all families. Inserted directly in the mystery of the Incarnation, the Family of Nazareth has its own special mystery. And in this mystery, as in the Incarnation, one finds a true fatherhood: *the human form of the family of the Son of God,* a true human family, formed by the divine mystery. *In this family, Joseph is the father: his fatherhood* is not one that derives from begetting offspring; but neither is it an "apparent" or merely "substitute" fatherhood. Rather, it is one that *fully shares in authentic human fatherhood* and the mission of a father in the family. This is a consequence of the hypostatic union: humanity taken up into the unity of the Divine Person of the Word-Son, Jesus Christ. Together with human nature, *all that is human, and especially the family* as the first dimension of man's existence in the world *is also taken up* in Christ. Within this context, Joseph's human fatherhood was also "taken up" in the mystery of Christ's Incarnation.

On the basis of this principle, the words which Mary spoke to the twelve-year-old Jesus in the Temple take on their full significance: *"Your father and I... have been looking for you."* This is no conventional phrase: Mary's words to Jesus show the complete reality of the Incarnation present in the mystery of the family of Nazareth. From the beginning, *Joseph accepted with the "obedience of faith"* his human fatherhood over

Jesus. And thus, following the light of the Holy Spirit who gives himself to human beings through faith, he certainly came to discover ever more fully *the indescribable gift that was his human fatherhood.*

IV Work as an expression of love

22. *Work was the daily expression of love in the life of the Family of Nazareth.* The Gospel specifies the kind of work Joseph did in order to support his family: he was a carpenter. This simple word sums up Joseph's entire life. For Jesus, these were hidden years, the years to which Luke refers after recounting the episode that occured in the Temple: "And he went down with them and came to Nazareth, and was obedient to them" (Lk 2:51). This *"submission"* or obedience of Jesus in the house of Nazareth should be *understood as a sharing in the work of Joseph.* Having learned the work of his presumed father, he was known as "the carpenter's son." If the Family of Nazareth is an example and model for human families in the order of salvation and holiness, so too, by analogy, is Jesus' work at the side of Joseph the carpenter. In our own day, the Church has emphasized this by instituting the liturgical memorial of St. Joseph the Worker on May 1. *Human work,* and especially manual labor, *receive special prominence in the Gospel.* Along with the humanity of the Son of God, work too has been taken up in the mystery of the Incarnation, *and has also been redeemed in a special way.* At the workbench where he plied his trade together with Jesus, Joseph brought human work closer to the mystery of the Redemption.

23. In the human growth of Jesus "in wisdom, age and grace," *the virtue of industriousness* played a notable role, since "work is a human good" which "transforms nature" and makes man "in a sense, more human."

The importance of work in human life demands that its meaning be known and assimilated in order to "help all people to come closer to God, the Creator and Redeemer, to participate in his salvific plan for man and the world, and to deepen... friendship with Christ in their lives, by accepting, through faith, a living participation in his threefold mission as Priest, Prophet and King."

24. What is crucially important here is the sanctification of daily life, a sanctification which each person must acquire according to his or her own state, and one which can be promoted according to a model accessible to all people: "St. Joseph is the model of those humble ones that Christianity raises up to great destinies;... he is the proof that in order to be a good and genuine follower of Christ, there is no need of great things — it is enough to have the common, simple and human virtues, but they need to be true and authentic."

V The primacy of the interior life

25. The same aura of silence that envelops everything else about Joseph also shrouds his work as a carpenter in the house of Nazareth. It is, however, *a silence that reveals in a special way the inner portrait* of the man. The Gospels speak exclusively of what Joseph "did." Still, they allow us to discover in his "actions" — shrouded in silence — as they are an aura of *deep contemplation.* This explains, for example, why St. Teresa of Jesus, the great reformer of the Carmelites, promoted the renewal of veneration to St. Joseph in Western Christianity.

26. The total sacrifice, whereby Joseph surrendered his whole existence to the demands of the Messiah's coming into his home, becomes understandable only in the light of his profound interior life. It was from

this interior life that "very singular commands and consolations came, bringing him also the logic and strength that belong to simple and clear souls, and giving him the power of making great decisions — such as the decision to put his liberty immediately at the disposition of the divine designs, to make over to them also his legitimate human calling, his conjugal happiness, to accept the conditions, the responsibility and the burden of a family, but, through an incomparable virginal love, to renounce that natural conjugal love that is the foundation and nourishment of the family."

This submission to God, this readiness of will to dedicate oneself to all that serves him, is really nothing less than that *exercise of devotion* which constitutes one expression of the virtue of religion.

27. The communion of life between Joseph and Jesus leads us to consider once again the mystery of the Incarnation, precisely in reference to the humanity of Jesus as the efficacious instrument of his divinity for the purpose of sanctifying man: "By virtue of his divinity, Christ's human actions were salvific for us, causing grace within us, either by merit or by a certain efficacy."

Among those actions, the Gospel writers highlight those which have to do with the Paschal Mystery, but they also underscore the importance of physical contact with Jesus for healing (cf. for example, Mk 1:41), and the influence Jesus exercised upon John the Baptist when they were both in their mothers' wombs (cf. Lk 1:41–44).

As we have seen, the apostolic witness did not neglect the story of Jesus' birth, his circumcision, his presentation in the Temple, his flight into Egypt and his hidden life in Nazareth. It recognized the "mystery" of grace present in each of these saving "acts," inasmuch as they all share the same source of love: the divinity of Christ. If through Christ's humanity this love shone on all mankind, the first beneficiaries were undoubtedly those whom the divine will had most intimately associated with itself: Mary, the Mother of Jesus, and Joseph, his presumed father.

Why should the "fatherly" love of Joseph not have had an influence upon the "filial" love of Jesus? And vice versa, why should the "filial" love of Jesus not have had an influence upon the "fatherly" love of Joseph, thus leading to a further deepening of their unique relationship? Those souls most sensitive to the impulses of divine love have rightly seen in Joseph a brilliant example of the interior life.

Furthermore, in Joseph, the apparent tension between the active and the contemplative life finds an ideal harmony that is only possible for those who possess the perfection of charity. Following St. Augustine's well-known distinction between the love of the truth (*caritas veritatis*) and the practical demands of love (*necessitas caritatis*), we can say that Joseph experienced both *love of the truth* — that pure contemplative love of the divine Truth which radiated from the humanity of Christ — and *the demands of love* — that equally pure and selfless love required for his vocation to safeguard and develop the humanity of Jesus, which was inseparably linked to his divinity.

VI Patron of the Church in our day

28. At a difficult time in the Church's history, Pope Pius IX, wishing to place her under the powerful patronage of the holy patriarch Joseph, declared him "Patron of the Catholic Church." For Pius IX this was no idle gesture, since by virtue of the sublime dignity which God has granted to his most faithful servant Joseph, "the Church, after the Blessed Virgin, his spouse, has always held him in great honor and showered him with praise, having recourse to him amid tribulations."

What are the reasons for such great confidence? Leo XIII explained it in this way: "The reasons why Saint Joseph must be considered the special patron of the Church, and the Church in turn draws exceeding hope from his care and patronage, chiefly arise from his having been the husband of Mary and the presumed father of Jesus..., Joseph was in his day the lawful and natural guardian, head and defender of the Holy Family.... It is thus fitting and most worthy of Joseph's dignity that, in the same way that he once kept unceasing holy watch over the family of Nazareth, so now does he protect and defend with his heavenly patronage the Church of Christ."

29. This patronage must be invoked as ever necessary for the Church, not only as a defense against all dangers, but also, and indeed primarily, as an impetus for her renewed commitment to evangelization in the world and to re-evangelization in those lands and nations where — as I wrote in the Apostolic Exhortation *Christifideles Laici* — "religion and the Christian life were formerly flourishing and... are now put to a hard test." In order to bring the first proclamation of Christ, or to bring it anew wherever it has been neglected or forgotten, the Church has need of special "power from on high" (cf. Lk 24:49; Acts 1:8): a gift of the Spirit of the Lord, a gift which is not unrelated to the intercession and example of his saints.

30. Besides trusting in Joseph's sure protection, the Church also trusts in his noble example, which transcends all individual states of life and serves as a model for the entire Christian community, whatever the condition and duties of each of its members may be.

As the Second Vatican Council's *Constitution on Divine Revelation* has said, the basic attitude of the entire Church must be that of "hearing the word of God with reverence," an absolute readiness to serve faithfully God's salvific will revealed in Jesus. Already at the beginning of human redemption, after Mary, we find the model of obedience made incarnate in Saint Joseph, the man known for having faithfully carried out God's commands.

Pope Paul VI invited us to invoke Joseph's patronage "as the Church has been wont to do in these recent times, for herself in the first place, with a spontaneous theological reflection on the marriage of divine and human action in the great economy of the Redemption, in which economy the first — the divine one — is wholly sufficient unto itself, while the second — the human action which is ours — though capable of nothing (cf. Jn 15:5), is never dispensed from a humble but conditional and ennobling collaboration. The Church also calls upon Joseph as her protector because of a profound and ever present desire to reinvigorate her ancient life with true evangelical virtues, such as shine forth in Saint Joseph."

31. The Church transforms these needs into prayer. Recalling that God wished to entrust the beginnings of our redemption to the faithful care of Saint Joseph, she asks God to grant that she may faithfully cooperate in the work of salvation; that she may receive the same faithfulness and purity of heart that inspired Joseph in serving the Incarnate Word; and that she may walk before God in the ways of holiness and Justice, following Joseph's example and through his intercession.

One hundred years ago, Pope Leo XIII had already exhorted the Catholic world to pray for the protection of Saint Joseph, Patron of the whole Church. The Encyclical Epistle *Quamquam Pluries* appealed to Joseph's "fatherly love... for the Child Jesus" and commended to him, as "the provident guardian of the divine family," "the beloved inheritance which Jesus Christ purchased by his blood." Since that time — as

I recalled at the beginning of this Exhortation — *the Church has implored the protection of St. Joseph* on the basis of "that sacred bond of charity which united him to the Immaculate Virgin Mother of God," and the Church has commended to Joseph all of her cares, including those dangers which threaten the human family.

Even *today* we have *many reasons to pray in a similar way:* "Most beloved father, dispel the evil of falsehood and sin... graciously assist us from heaven in our struggle with the powers of darkness... and just as once you saved the Child Jesus from mortal danger, so now defend God's Holy Church from the snares of her enemies and from all adversity." Today we still have *good reason to commend everyone to Saint Joseph.*

32. It is my heartfelt wish that these reflections on the person of Saint Joseph will renew in us the prayerful devotion which my predecessor called for a century ago. Our prayers and *the very person of Joseph have renewed significance for the Church in our day* in light of the Third Christian Millennium.

The Second Vatican Council made all of us sensitive once again to the "great things which God has done," and to that *"economy of salvation"* of which Saint Joseph was a special minister. Commending ourselves, then, to the protection of him to whose custody God "entrusted his greatest and most precious treasures," *let us at the same time learn from him how to be servants of the "economy of salvation."* May Saint Joseph become for all of us an exceptional teacher in the service of *Christ's saving mission,* a mission which is the responsibility of each and every member of the Church: husbands and wives, parents, those who live by the work of their hands or by any other kind of work, those called to the contemplative life and those called to the apostolate.

This just man, who bore within himself the entire heritage of the Old Covenant, was also *brought into the "beginning" of the New and Eternal Covenant in Jesus Christ.* May he show us the paths of this saving Covenant as we stand at the threshold of the next Millennium, in which there must be a continuation and further development of the "fullness of time" that belongs to the ineffable mystery of the Incarnation of the Word.

May Saint Joseph obtain for the Church and for the world, as well as for each of us, the blessing of the Father, Son and the Holy Spirit.

Given at Rome, in St. Peter's, on 15 August — the Solemnity of the Assumption of the Blessed Virgin Mary — in the year 1989, the eleventh of my Pontificate.

Joannes Paulus pp. II

This document brings to date many thoughts that have been proposed over the ages, thus adding those important threads to a still incomplete tapestry.

Fifth International Symposium

The Fifth International Symposium to discuss St. Joseph was held September 17–24, 1989 in Mexico. The opening address was delivered by the Archbishop of Mexico in the Basilica of Our Lady of Guadalupe followed by a magnificent Eucharistic concelebration presided over by the apostolic delegate to Mexico, Mgr. Girolamo Prigione. Although this basilica, dedicated to Mary, is one of the biggest in the world, it could not accommodate the throng which had gathered to participate in this solemn inauguration.

About fifty speakers took turns to speak on the theology and worship of St. Joseph as experienced during the 18th Century. Many amongst them were from

Mexico and Central America but many others were from Canada, the United States, Italy, Spain, Poland, Malta, France and Belgium. A true gathering of nations where a gift for languages was of great benefit. Several speakers recapitulated how the writers of the 18th Century had presented the providential mission and the spiritual figure of St. Joseph in the comments on the Scriptures, in theology, in religious literature and in sermons. Others showed how, over the course of this same century, the people of God worshipped the husband of Mary through the texts of the liturgy, by various acts of popular devotion and by the contemplation of works of art.

During the symposium, people could visit three expositions featuring the worship of Saint Joseph: one of which featured many sculptures of Mary's spouse; another featured paintings and the third was an exhibition of old books about the head of the Holy Family.

1990 and Real Estate

The depressed Real Estate market of 1990 brought St. Joseph to the secular press. It was with mixed emotions that we read the article on the front page of the Sunday edition of the "Philadelphia Inquirer" (*"Another Sale by St. Joseph,"* 9/23/90 by staff writer Robin Clark). There was also interest on why this article was not assigned to the Real Estate section instead of page one as the content deals with Real Estate.

Those of us who pray to St. Joseph to intercede to the Good God for our worthy intentions know that our prayers will be heard and answered. We therefore have reason to resent referral to St. Joseph's statue as a good luck charm only to share equal status with a four-leaf clover or rabbit's foot. What irked those with great confidence in St. Joseph the most, were the suggestions, by those untutored, that he must be buried head down with his toes pointing toward the building. How ridiculous!

The practice of placing a medal or statue of St. Joseph to obtain property has been going on for years. Br. Alderic, a companion of Br. André, buried a medal of St. Joseph on Mount Royal in anticipation of the Holy Cross Order securing the property for St. Joseph. Br. André never lost confidence that an Oratory would one day occupy the mountain. In simple faith, he placed a small statue of St. Joseph, facing out the window of Notre Dame College, looking at the mountain with full knowledge that one day a home for St. Joseph would occupy the site.

Perhaps there was a different reason for the page one position. After speaking with Robin Clark of the Inquirer staff, he answered that the editorial staff felt it was well written and would have great public interest. Since its first appearance, the article went out through the Inquirer's national wire service and was subsequently picked up by the Associated Press who did their story and according to Robin Clark, it has appeared in many prominent newspapers such as the Chicago Tribune, USA Today, The Wall Street Journal as well as Newsweek Magazine.

All of this comes down to making St. Joseph more prominent to millions of people. Regardless of the intention of the writers of the many articles that appeared, no one can deny that St. Joseph has received the acclaim that he richly deserves.

To speculate what the future will bring would be impossible. God's ultimate plan is unfolding as each additional thread is added to this yet unfinished tapestry.

Prayers and Devotions

We are reminded that each Wednesday and the entire Month of March are dedicated to St. Joseph. We should perform some pious act especially at this time and in particular during the nine days preceeding March 19th and on the First Wednesday of each month. We are also asked to include St. Joseph in the prayers during the month of October. The following are some of the prayers and devotions dedicated to St. Joseph.

PERPETUAL NOVENA
IN THANKSGIVING

O God most bounteous, Who have created everything out of love and Who govern the world through your Divine Providence, we praise and thank You for the countless benefits You have shed upon us, and particularly for the outstanding privilege of Saint Joseph's protection.

With the help of Your grace, we propose to show ourselves worthy of his blessings by treading in his footsteps, constantly striving to please You in all our words and deeds, that we may always justifiably claim to be your true children, brothers and sisters of Jesus and sons and daughters of Mary. Amen.

THE LITANY OF SAINT JOSEPH

V. Lord, have mercy. **R. Christ, have mercy.**
V. Lord, have mercy. Christ, hear us. **R. Christ, graciously hear us.**

V. God the Father of Heaven, **R. have mercy on us.**
V. God the Son, Redeemer of the world, **R. have mercy on us.**

V. God the Holy Spirit, **R. have mercy on us.**
V. Holy Trinity, One God, **R. have mercy on us.**
V. Holy Mary, **R. pray for us.**
St. Joseph,
Illustrious Son of David,
Splendor of Patriarchs,
Spouse of the Mother of God,
Chaste protector of the Virgin,
Foster-father of the Son of God,
Zealous defender of Christ,
Head of the Holy Family,
Joseph most just,
Joseph most pure,
Joseph most prudent,
Joseph most courageous,
Joseph most obedient,
Joseph most faithful,
Mirror of patience,
Lover of poverty,
Model of workmen,
Glory of domestic life,
Guardian of virgins,
Mainstay of families,
Comfort of the afflicted,
Hope of the sick,
Patron of the dying,
Terror of demons,
Protector of the Holy Church,

Lamb of God, who take away the sins of the world,
R. Spare us, Lord.
Lamb of God, who take away the sins of the world,
R. Hear us, Lord.
Lamb of God, who take away the sins of the world,
R. Have mercy on us.
V. He has made him master of His house.
R. And ruler of His possessions.

V. Let us pray **R. O God, who in your loving providence chose Blessed Joseph to be the spouse of your most Holy Mother, give to us the favor of having him for our intercessor in heaven whom on earth we venerate as our Protector. You, who live and reign forever and ever. Amen.**

MEMORARE TO SAINT JOSEPH

Remember, O most chaste Spouse of the Virgin Mary, that never was it known that anyone who asked for your help and sought your intercession was left unaided.

Full of confidence in your power, I hasten to you and beg your protection. Listen, O foster-father of the Redeemer, to my humble prayer, and in your goodness hear and answer me. Amen.

TO OBTAIN A SPECIAL FAVOR

O Blessed Saint Joseph, tender-hearted father, faithful guardian of Jesus, chaste spouse of the Mother of God, I pray to you to join with me in praising God the Father through His divine Son who died on the cross and rose again to give us sinners new life. Through the holy Name of Jesus, pray with us that we may obtain from the ternal Father the favor we ask for. . . .

We, who have been unfaithful to the unfailing love of God the Father; beg of Jesus mercy for us his brothers and sisters. Amid the spendors of God's loving presence, do not forget the sorrows of those who weep. By your prayers and those of your most holy Spouse, our Blessed Lady, may the love of Jesus answer our call of confident hope. Amen.

DEVOTION IN HONOR OF THE SEVEN SORROWS AND SEVEN JOYS OF SAINT JOSEPH

I
Joseph's worries during his engagement
Matthew 1:18–24

Meditation: O Saint Joseph, we can scarcely imagine your affliction and your anguish when you were aware that Mary your betrothed was expecting a child whose origin was unknown to you. Your confidence in her prevented you from condemning her and your righteousness from putting her to shame. Staring into such a great mystery, you considered whether it was better to go your way and it was with extreme pain that you were about to send her away in secret, believing that your union with her was forever doomed.

But the news the Angel delivered in your sleep allowed you to understand that the Messiah had just become flesh by the Holy Spirit of the Virgin Mary; not only was Mary blessed by God, but you also were to keep her as your wife and Jesus, the Son of God, as your son. With what joy and respect you must have responded to the Angel's order and with what bliss you were ready to live with Mary and Jesus, the two most holy beings that ever existed.

Prayer: With this example before our eyes, O Saint Joseph, we ask you to grant us that may understand that in our lives great graces may come after great trials, and that when sorrow visits us it does not mean that God forsakes us, but rather that He is near, preparing us solace after suffering, in His goodness.

Our Father. Hail Mary. Glory be.

II
The Birth of Jesus in Bethlehem and the Adoration of the Shepherds
Luke 2:1–20

Meditation: O Saint Joseph, your surprise and sorrow must have been great on your way to Bethlehem to have been refused a place in the inn, just at the time when Mary, about to give birth to the Messiah, was in need of rest and privacy. Undoubtedly, it must have taken you much faith and hope to accept such miserable conditions for the birth of the Son of God, remarkable for its destitution and the neglect of men. But your sorrow was changed into joy and your suffering into hope, when you saw the shepherds, sent by the angels, arrive at the manger to adore the Son of God.

Prayer: O Saint Joseph, obtain for us the grace to understand that if our faith is often put to the test, we must meet all obstacles with strength and perseverance, and that God reaches out for men not in riches or pomp but in poverty and humility.

Our Father. Hail Mary. Glory be.

III
Presentation of Jesus in the Temple
Luke 2: 22–40

O Saint Joseph, when you went up to the Temple with the Virgin Mary and her son, Jesus, you wanted to fulfill both the prescriptions for the purification of the Mother and the offering of the Child. It was a great joy when you saw that Simeon and Anna, by prophetic inspiration, recognized the Messiah in Jesus and sang his praise and his future glory. But, just as for Mary, a sword pierced through your soul when you heard that Jesus must fulfill His mission and save men through suffering and that He was destined to bring

about the fall and the rise of many in Israel.
Prayer: O Saint Joseph, by these joys and sorrows of yours, help us to recognize that God may at times take away the gifts He has bestowed on us, and teach us to bless and love Him, even when He sends tribulations after rejoicings.

Our Father. Hail Mary. Glory be.

IV
The Visit of the Wise Men and Flight into Egypt
Matthew 2:1–15

Meditation: O Saint Joseph, after the purification of Mary and the presenting of Jesus in the Temple, you had the joy of seeing another testimony to the divinity and mission of Jesus. The wise men from the East brought before Him their gifts and homage. So, after the humble shepherds, representing the Jewish people, had come to worship Jesus, now the wise men, standing for all the nations, had been called. But the sword of affliction was drawn. Herod, hearing of a newborn King of the Jews and fearing for his rank decided to put the child to death. Warned in a dream, you had to leave for a foreign country with Mary and the Child.
Prayer: O Saint Joseph, we beseech you, help us to imitate you wholeheartedly when we are subjected, against our will and fancy, to the mysterious and disarming action of Divine Providence. Make us understand that "the ways of God are not our ways", and that what we think wise and essential may appear to Him as silly and dangerous to our souls. Grant that we accept, as you did, these contradictions that escape our understanding but can lead us back to the way of grace and salvation.

Our Father. Hail Mary. Glory be.

V
Jesus lost and found
Luke 2:41–52

Meditation: O Saint Joseph, how troubled and anguished you must have been when, returning from Jerusalem, you became aware with Mary that the Child God had entrusted to you, was no longer with you.

What eagerness in your search for Him during three days! What happiness in finding Him in the Temple and coming back to Nazareth where He lived with you in peace and subjection, advancing in favor and wisdom and working at your side.

Prayer: Obtain for us the grace, O Saint Joseph, to seek our Savior with your eagerness and Mary's. Teach us to find him in the temple in the midst of teachers, that is, in the Eucharist and in the teaching of God's Church. Make us experience the happiness in living with him in peace and conformably to God's will, that we also may grow in favor and in wisdom.

Our Father. Hail Mary. Glory be.

VI
The joys and sorrows of Joseph at work
Matthew 13:53–55

Meditation: O Saint Joseph, when we learn from the Gospel that you were a carpenter, we understand that your life was spent in the humble and patient labor of the workers of all times. In this daily work which you did wholeheartedly to earn the living of the Holy Family, you surely met with joy and sorrow, trials and solace. Hours of success and gain were followed by hours of sickness and fatigue. You met generous and polite customers, but also exacting and churlish ones. Some chores were pleasant and easy, others difficult and thankless. But in every situation you did your best and fulfilled your obligations.

Prayer: Teach us, O Saint Joseph, to fulfill our daily tasks with perfection, to work for God and not only for men, with care and honesty, and to accept contradictions and rejoicings in a Christian spirit.

Our Father. Hail Mary. Glory be.

VII
Death of St. Joseph
John 19:26–27

Meditation: O Saint Joseph, we do not know the circumstances of your death. But since Jesus, dying on the Cross, asked His beloved disciple to look after Mary, the Church has always believed that you had the joy of dying in the arms of Jesus and Mary. That is why the Church sees in you the patron of the dying. After a holy life you died a happy death, and after the trials of this life, you experienced the bliss of heaven where now you enjoy the presence of Jesus and Mary.

Prayer: O Saint Joseph, who experienced the joy of dying in the embrace of Jesus and Mary and whom Christians honor as the patron and comforter of the dying, we call on you today for your protection at the last moment of our life. May we die the death of the just, and in order to merit such a grace, may we live like you in the presence of the Lord and of the Virgin Mary, so as to share in the Redemption when we appear for the judgement of the Lord.

Our Father. Hail Mary. Glory be.

TO THE PROTECTOR OF HOLY CHURCH

O Saint Joseph, husband of the Virgin Mary and virginal father of Christ Jesus, you have been charged with the protection of the Universal Church, so that you might extend to all the children of the Kingdom the care you first took of the members of the Holy Family.

From the high heavens where you are now living with Jesus and Mary, be the protector and guide of the people of God walking toward its eternal goal.

Bring together from the four corners of the earth the elect of the Kingdom, so that they may live united in one Body. Lead all Christians to the union of charity in the unity of faith.

Secure for the Holy Father, for all our bishops united to him, and for all of us who make up with them the Church of God, the graces of light and strength to understand always more clearly the teaching of Jesus Christ.

Sustain those among us who are fervent, wake up the lukewarm, uphold those who are in distress, convert the sinners, heal the sick and comfort the afflicted. Make the peace of God shine upon us, so that we may help establish His rule over the world in an atmosphere of freedom. Amen.

FOR THE POPE

Saint Joseph, Patron of the Universal Church, please help and support our Holy Father the Pope in his work as supreme Pastor of all the faithful; obtain for him the graces and the light of the Holy Spirit, so that he may be for all a model of virtue, of holiness, and that sustained by the force from on high, he may govern the Church with kindness and goodness, with wisdom, strength and righteousness. Pray that he may enjoy perfect health and live only for God and the salvation of souls, according to the example of Christ Himself, who has loved us and given His life to save us. Amen.

FOR PRIESTLY AND RELIGIOUS VOCATIONS

Saint Joseph, patron of the Church, we ask you to intercede before God, so that in our days as always in the Church, many young people be attracted to the service of souls and to the ideal of evangelical perfection.

Already among Christian nations, the faithful desire to better understand and practice the virtues preached by Christ; and among non-Christian peoples, a great number of men and women of good will hear the call of faith and want to receive the message of peace.

Please pray on our behalf that the Master of the harvest send workers to his vineyard. Obtain for us many priestly and religious vocations, vocations of missionaries, educators and contemplatives that correspond to the immense needs of the world today and that are fully dedicated to the service of the Lord and of His Church. Amen.

FOR THE SANCTIFICATION OF LABOR

Glorious Saint Joseph, model of all workers, obtain for me the grace to work in the spirit of thanksgiving and joy. Let me consider it an honor to use and develop the gifts received from God. Aid me to work in order, peace, moderation and patience without ever avoiding weariness and trials; to work conscientiously, preferring my duty to my inclinations; to work in spirit of penance for the expiation of my sins. Help me to work above all for the glory of God and not for any selfish reasons, and to keep before my eyes the account I must give of time lost and work badly done. Watch over me and give me the strength to imitate you in order that I may obtain the reward of those who work for God. Amen.

FOR THE UNEMPLOYED

O Saint Joseph, we pray to you for those who are out of work, for those who want to earn their living or support their families.

You who are the patron of workers; grant that unemployment may vanish from our ranks; that all those who are ready to work may put their strength and abilities in serving their fellow men and earn a just salary.

You are the patron of families; do not let those who have children to support and raise lack the necessary means. Have pity on our brothers and sisters held down in unemployment and poverty because of sickness or social disorders. Help our political leaders and captains of industry find new and just solutions; may each and every one have the joy of contributing, according to his or her abilities, to the common prosperity by an honorable livelihood. Grant that we may all share together in the abundant goods God has given us and that we may help underprivileged countries. Amen.

FOR MY VOCATION

Saint Joseph, during your earthly life, you were always faithful to whatever designs God has planned for you. I, in turn, also wish to collaborate with the Lord who is at present concerned with the world. Help me to know in what state of life I may best participate in His action. Make me attentive to the signs He will give me during these years of preparation for my future. Once I have discovered His call, help me still further to enter, with perfect fidelity, in the project that I shall have formulated with Him. Amen.

AN ACT OF CONSECRATION

Saint Joseph, head of the Holy Family, God chose you among men to be the protector of the Christ Child and the guardian of the Virgin Mary. To you whom the Church honors as her patron we joyfully come to consecrate ourselves and to be your adopted children. We feel the great need of your kind protection. Our weakness and proneness to evil would cause us to perish, but for your protecting arm. Saint Joseph, from heaven where you reign with Jesus and Mary, look upon us who promise to follow your example. Grant that after fulfilling our Christian duties on earth, we may have the happiness of dying with the names of Jesus, Mary and Joseph on our lips. Amen.

PRAYER OF MARCH 19TH

May the merits of your most holy Mother's spouse help us, we beseech you, O Lord, that through his intercession we may receive what we cannot obtain by our own efforts. Who lives and reigns, with God the Father, in the unity of the Holy Spirit, God, world without end. Amen.

PRAYER FOR MAY 1ST

O God, the creator of all things, who framed the law of labor for the human race, graciously grant that, by the example and patronage of Saint Joseph, we may do the work you assign us and earn the reward you promise. Through our Lord Jesus Christ, your Son, who lives and reigns with you in the unity of the Holy Spirit, God, world without end. Amen.

PRAYER FOR OCTOBER

(For text see page 114)

IN SICKNESS

Merciful Saint Joseph, the omnipotence of Jesus is in your hands. Nothing is impossible to you. You have but to say a word and our beloved invalid will be cured. O comforter of those who invoke you with confidence, do not reject our plea. The sick have a special right to your tender compassion. Alleviate, we beseech you, the pains of the one we recommend to you. . . . Obtain for him or her the grace to sanctify his or her sufferings through the patience and total submission to God's holy Will. But moreover, crown your blessings by granting him or her a cure, along with the grace of leading a saintly life wholly pleasing to God. O beloved Saint Joseph, let not our prayers rise in vain, but deign, by this additional favor, to increase our confidence in you and our gratitude towards Divine Goodness. Amen.

FOR A HAPPY DEATH

Saint Joseph, who had the joy of dying between Jesus and Mary, and whom all Christians honor as the patron and comforter of the dying, I call upon your protection for the last instants of my life. May I die the death of the just, and to obtain such a grace, may I live as you in the presence of the Lord and of the Virgin Mary, so as to share in the Redemption when I also will have to appear before God. Amen.

FOR OUR FAMILY CIRCLE

Great Saint Joseph, who was chosen by God to be the head of the holiest family ever to grace the earth, kindly look down upon us and extend your special protection to our home. Model of the most lively faith and of all virtues, obtain for all the members of our family the grace to resist the temptations and allurements of the world and to live close to the Lord. May we ever remain bound together by the ties of true Christian love and taste the peace that Jesus has promised His true disciples. Grant that we may all work together and love one another as children of God, in order to fulfill our role in the great family of the Church. Amen.

A CHRISTIAN HUSBAND'S PRAYER

Saint Joseph, spouse of the Virgin Mary and virginal father of Christ Jesus, patron of families and protector of the Church, grant me the light and the strength I need to fulfill as a Christian my many duties.

Help me to understand and love the woman I have chosen before God as life's companion and helper in my task here on earth. Grant me tact and patience, good spirits and confidence in all my relationships with her. May I be to her a friend and a father, a guide and a confidant, a companion and a helper. Grant that I may give her not only financial support but also the assurance of my presence, that I may expect from her not only the comforts of the body but also the joys of the heart and the spirit; may I be her instructor in temperal as well as spiritual matters. May I enjoy her presence not only in pleasure and relaxation but in work and prayer. May I discover in her the fresh spring of affection and attention, of poetry and prayer that God has placed by my side, to remind me of Him and the beauty of His works.

Grant that I respect her likes and opinions by not holding back the freedom she is entitled to; may I help her come into her own in peace and confidence by encouraging her in her efforts and progress. May I always remember that we are partners for eternity and shall stay united in God after death, when all tears will be wiped away, all misunderstanding removed and all faults forgiven. For then we shall receive before God, forever, the reward of our fidelity and love on earth. Amen.

IN AFFLICTION

Saint Joseph, solace of the afflicted, you whom nobody has called on in vain, grant me your fatherly protection. At this moment I am in a dire situation and I pray to you in all confidence. You are so close to God, pray for me, intercede for me. I believe that as a father you can help me in my difficulties. I ask of you the grace to accept them, to go beyond them with the same strength that helped you in going forward in the middle of your sorrows. Help me to carry my cross without envy or bitterness. And if it is God's will, deliver me from this trial.

O Saint Joseph, I beseech you, hear my prayer; have pity on your child in distress. Be favorable to me and hear my prayer. Amen.

PRAYER TO SAINT JOSEPH FOR MARRIED COUPLES

Dear Saint Joseph, humble and just husband of Mary, grant us your powerful intercession that especially husbands and wives may be faithful to their sacred vows. Inspire them with the desire to be not only just but also charitable toward each other.

In imitation of your behavior, may they always endeavor to do God's will. Let them realize the great responsibility that is theirs with respect to their partner, especially in what concerns their growth in holiness as willed by God.

When they have children, let them realize that there is no greater good for them upon earth than to do the best in raising those children as children of God, destined to live in perfect happiness with God for all eternity. May they follow your example and that of Mary, your spouse, and above all the example of the One Who lived so long with you and was the Son of God made Man. Amen.

A FATHER'S PRAYER

Saint Joseph, head of the Holy Family, grant me the spiritual gifts and virtues I need to fulfill my duties as head of the family entrusted to me by God.

With the help of my wife, may I discharge the God given responsibilities with devotion and respect, with faith and charity. Following your example, may I bring to my daily task the care and respect that will really make it a collaboration to God's work and a true service to men, my brothers.

In spite of social conditions and spells of sickness, may I earn enough to supply my family with food and lodging, clothing and education, in the joy of a hearth safe from distress.

Teach me the true virtues of a husband and Christian educator. As you went to great pains to feed and educate Jesus, the child of God entrusted to your care, grant that I may bring up my children with love and firmness, with intelligence and tact; that I may pray with them and explain to them, when and how I must, their obligations as Christians, by word and act; may I stay calm and patient when they fail and err, without fear of admonishing and correcting them when I must. May I give to each one, according to his or her character and personality, the necessary incentives, with special attention and affection. May I not be too often absent from home, since my wife and children require my presence.

O Saint Joseph, grant that I may always live as a true Christian, and observe the fidelity, the love and devotion I owe to my wife and children, since I have received from God the difficult and wonderful mission of leading them all to His Kingdom. Amen.

PRAYER OF THE ASSOCIATES

Note: The Associates are those dedicated to The Work of Saint Joseph by "spreading devotion to the holy patriarch, and the imitation of his virtues." The following prayer is said on Wednesday, in private or in community.

"O Joseph! Who by your fidelity to the inspiration of Heaven, merited, in the midst of hard labor, the contempt of the world and the trials of this life, to receive from the Holy Spirit the title of Just, and from God the Father the care of Jesus, His Divine Son, and Mary, the Queen of virgins; we implore of you, now that you are all-powerful with God, to remember us, who still languish in this valley of tears, exposed to the snares of cruel enemies. Obtain for us a contempt for the false goods of this world, victory over our passions, an unbounded zeal in the service of God, a tender confidence in Jesus, your adopted Son, and in Mary, your spouse. O Joseph! Be our guide, our patron, our defender at the hour of death. We beg this of you, by the love which you bear to Jesus and Mary. We beseech you to ask the same graces for all those who have associated themselves to us to spread devotion to you. Listen to their prayers, assist their efforts, and obtain, in reward for their zeal, that they may one day be united around your throne at the feet of Jesus and Mary. Amen.

"Sacred Heart of Jesus, have mercy on us."

"Immaculate Heart of Mary, pray for us."

"St. Joseph, pray for us."

Add an Our Father and a Hail Mary for each special intention.

BIBLIOGRAPHY and REFERENCE SOURCES

1) Baldwin, Lou. A CALL TO SANCTITY: The Formation and Life of Mother Katherine Drexel, Philadelphia, Pa: The Catholic Standard and Times, 1987.
2) Binet, Pere. THE DIVINE FAVORS GRANTED TO ST. JOSEPH, Rockford, Illinois: Tan books and Publishers Inc., 1983.
3) Bram, Leon L., Editorial Director. FUNK & WAGNALLS NEW ENCYCLOPEDIA, New York: Funk & Wagnalls, Inc., 1979.
4) Doheny, W. J., C.S.C. ST. ANASTASIA, THE SAINT AND HER BASILICA IN ROME, 1956.
5) EXPOSITION sur SAINT JOSEPH, inauguree le 30 juillet 1955.
6) Eymard, Blessed Peter Julian. MONTH OF JOSEPH, New York: The Sentinel Press, 1948.
7) Faber, Frederick William. FOOT OF THE CROSS or THE SORROWS OF MARY, Baltimore: John Murphy & Co., 1857.
8) Faber, Frederick William. THE BLESSED SACRAMENT, or, THE WORKS AND WAYS OF GOD, Baltimore: John Murphy & Co., 1855.
9) Filas, Francis L., S.J. JOSEPH: THE MAN CLOSEST TO JESUS, Boston: Daughter of St. Paul, 1962.
10) Filas, Francis L., S.J. ST. JOSEPH AFTER VATICAN II, Youngtown, Arizona: Cogan Productions, 1981.
11) LE PATRONAGE de ST. JOSEPH, Montreal: St. Joseph's Oratory, 1956.
12) L'OBSERVATORE ROMANO, weekly edition in English, October 30, 1989.
13) Levy, Rosalie Marie. JOSEPH THE JUST MAN, Boston: Daughters of St. Paul, 1955.
14) Marchi, John de, I. M. C. MOTHER OF CHRIST CRUSADE, Billings, Montana: Mother of Christ Crusade, Inc.

15) Neary, Tom. I COMFORTED THEM IN SORROW, KNOCK 1879–1979, County Mayo, Ireland: Custodians of Knock Shrine, 1979.

16) NEW CATHOLIC ENCYCLOPEDIA.

17) OLD ST. JOSEPH'S CHURCH, Rectory, Philadelphia, Pa.

18) O'Rafferty, Rev. Nicholas. DISCOURSES ON SAINT JOSEPH, Milwaukee: The Bruce Publishing Company, 1951.

19) Patrignani, Giuseppe Antonio, S.J. A MANUAL OF PRACTICAL DEVOTION TO THE GLORIOUS PATRIARCH ST. JOSEPH, Rockford, Illinois: Tan Books, 1982.

20) Rondet, Henri, S.J. SAINT JOSEPH, New York: P.J. Kenedy & Sons, 1956.

21) Suarez, Federico. JOSEPH OF NAZARETH, Manila: SinagTala Publishers, Inc., 1985.

22) PREMIER SYMPOSIUM INTERNATIONAL St. Joseph durant Les Quinze Premiers Sicles de L'Eglise, Montreal: St. Joseph's Oratory, 1971.

23) DEUXIME SYMPOSIUM INTERNATIONAL St. Joseph L'Epoque de la Renaissance (1450–1600), Montreal: St. Joseph's Oratory, 1977.

24) TROISIME SYMPOSIUM INTERNATIONAL St. Joseph au XVII Sicle, Montreal: St. Joseph's Oratory, 1981.

25) QUARTIME SYMPOSIUM INTERNATIONAL Prsence de St. Joseph au XVII Sicle, Montreal: St. Joseph's Oratory, 1987.

26) Thompson, Edward Healy, M.A. THE LIFE AND GLORIES OF SAINT JOSEPH, Rockford, Illinois: Tan Books and Publishers, 1888.

27) Van de Putte, Rev. Walter, C.S.SP. FOLLOWING SAINT JOSEPH, New York: Catholic Book Publishing Co, 1980.

28) Varkey, P.A., M.A. ST. JOSEPH, ENVOY OF THE HEAVENLY FATHER AT NAZARETH, India: Mar Mathews Press Muvattupuzha, 1987.

29) Translated by Rev. Richard J. Cleary, O.S.B.

REFERENCES

(Reference Sources are listed by # and page)
(Any references not so noted are from St. Joseph's Oratory)

Chapter 1

"The New American Bible", St. Joseph Edition

Chapter 2

Page 16 thru 19: #3 #18 #20
Page 19: St. Justin – #16 #26 p.100; 138
Page 20: St. Anastasia – #3 #4 #26 p.452
Page 21: St. Athanasius – #16 #26 p.89; 450
St. Ephrem – #13 p.152
St. Ambrose – #18 p.207 #26 p.72; 130
Page 22: St. John Chrysostom – #6 p.21 #20 p.11; 55 #21 p.35 #26 p.391; 429; 435 #28 p.50
Page 25: St. Augustine – #18 p.28; 75 149; 189 #20 p.11–12 #21 p.45 #26 p.315
Page 27: St. Jerome – #4 p.40 #18, p.13; 37; 58 #20 p.9 #26 p.89; 410; 452
Page 29: St. Peter Chrysologus – #26 p.92

Chapter 3

Page 30: Venerable Bede – #18 p.150 #26 p.409
Page 31: St. Joseph the Hymnographer – #26 p.451
Page 32: St. Peter Damian – #26 p.90
St. Bernard – #2 p.87 #6 p.7; 14 #9 p.57; 495 #20 p.17; 57 #26 p.19; 428
Page 33: Church of Bologna – #26 p.451 #28 p.112
St. Albert the Great – #26 p.123; 429; 436; 437; 442; 443
Page 34: St. Bonaventure – #28 p.87
St. Thomas Aquinas – #13 p.147 #18 p.37; 208; 213 #20 p.22 #26 p.41–42
Page 35: Holy House of Loreto – #13 p.111 #18
Page 37: St. Margaret of Cortona – #13 p.152
Page 38: St. Bridget of Sweden – #13 p.148 #26 p.432; 439
Page 39: St. Bernardine of Siena – #6 p.25; 28; 31; 40; 95 #13 p.145 #18 p.181; 191 #20 p.70–74 #26 p.61; 129; 415; 423; 454 #28 p.88
Page 45: John Cardinal Gerson – #20 #28 p.88–89; 112–113
Page 46: Pierre Cardinal D'Ailly – #26 p.479; 480 #28 p.90; 113
Page 47: End of Middle Ages – #20 p.21

Chapter 4

Page 48: Bernardine de Bustis – #26 p.12; 43; 469
Pope Sixtus IV – #9 p.537 #27 p.23
Page 50: Early 1500's – #26 p.444
Raphael – #20 p.235 illust. #20 p.151
Dominican Order (1508) – #28 p.115
Page 51: Isidore Isolano – #6 p.91 #20, p.26 #26 p.480; 505 #28 p.91; 92
Page 52: Bernardine of Loredo – #21 p.31–32
St. Teresa of Jesus – #3 #6 p.107 #13 p.145–147 #20 p.93 #26 p.435; 466–467
St. Teresa of Avila, Baglioni 1723, p.22
Page 55: Council of Trent – #10 p.103

232

	Francisco Suarez – #18 p.186 St. Lawrence of Brindisi – #28 p.40; 54–55
Page 56:	Brother Alexis – #26 p.434 Folk literature – #28 p.92; 93

Chapter 5

Page 57:	St. Francis de Sales – #6 p.64; 68; 72; 76; 103 #18 p.181 #20, p.29; 78 #26 p.416 #28 p.42; 94
Page 60:	Jean de Bolland – #3 vol. 4, p.63 #3 vol. 21, p.39 #18 p.38 #26 p.410 Venerable Mary of Agreda – #13 p.150–152 #18 p.45; 181 #20 p.31 #28 p.61
Page 62:	Jacques-Benigne Bossuet – #6 p.10; 48 #20 p.30; 95; 127
Page 66:	May 8, 1621 – #27 p.23 Carmelite Chapter – #26 p.473 17th Century growth – #28 p.95
Page 67:	December 6, 1670 – #13 p.168; 169
Page 68:	August 17, 1678 – #9 p.634 1679 and 1680 – #10 p.104 Carmelite's (1689) – #26 p.473 St. Leonard of Port Maurice – #18 p.150 #26 p.416

Chapter 6

Page 69:	Alphonsus Liguori – #6 p.55 #13 p.143–144 #18 p.207 #20 p.151 #28 p.97
Page 73:	Fr. Alban Butler – #20 p.148 Pope Clement XI #27 p.23 China – #28 p.99 Old St. Joseph's Church – #17 #28 p.99

Page 74:	1735 – #26 p.473 Pope Bendict XIV – #26 p.453 Frances Allen – #13 p.105 #28 p.99 Oratory Magazine, 1927, p.183

Chapter 7

Page 78:	St. Madaleine Sophie Barat – #13 p.147–148
Page 79:	St. Pierre Eymard – #6 #13 p.149–150
Page 82:	Little Sisters of the Poor – #13 various pages; Holy Family Home, Philadelphia, Pa.
Page 84:	Fr. William Frederick Faber – #6 p.34; 36; 43; 52; 58; 85 #7 #8 p.186–193 #20 p.161
Page 89:	Pius IX (1847) – #9 p.634 John Henry Cardinal Newman – #3 #20 p.175
Page 92:	Pius IX (1854) – #9 p.634 Herbert Cardinal Vaughan – #20 p. 203
Page 95:	Bernadette of Lourdes – Oratory Magazine, 1947 p.65

Chapter 8

Page 96:	Pope Pius IX (1870) – #9 p.634; 578–581 #27 p.23
Page 98:	Pope Pius IX (Inclytum Patriarcham) – #9 p.634; 581–583
Page 100:	Miracle Staircase– #13 p.199; Josephite Mission Newsletter
Page 102:	June 14, 1873 – #9 p.634 May 11, 1878 – #9 p.635 Cap-de-la-Madeleine – #5 p.58; St. Joseph's Oratory
Page 103:	Our Lady of Knock – #14 p.19–26
Page 105:	Canon Antonio Vitali – #26 p.479; 483
Page 106:	September 19, 1883 and January 6, 1884 – #9 p.635 1884 – #9 p.673 #27 p.23

233

Page 107:	1887 – #28 p.118 August 15, 1889 (Quamquam Pluries) – #9 p.647 #10 p.104 #29
Page 115:	Neminem Fugit (June 14, 1892) – #9 p.596–600
Page 117:	August 15, 1892 – #9 p.454 #10 p.104 #29
Page 118:	St. Theresa of Lisieux – St. Joseph's Oratory, Montreal Bl. Mother Katherine Drexel – #1 p.31

Chapter 9

Page 125:	Alexis H. M. Cardinal Lepicier – #9 p.622 #20 p.208–211
Page 127:	Pope Pius X (March 18, 1909) – #9 p.635
Page 129	Fr. Frederic – Oratory Magazine, Sept. 1988
Page 130:	Pope Pius X (1911, 1912 & 1913) – #9 p.635
Page 131:	Our Lady of Fatima – #14 #29 #5 p.59
Page 133:	Pope Benedict XV (1917 and 1919) – #9 p.635 Bonum Sane – #9 p.600–604 #13 p.182 #27 p.24
Page 138:	1921 – #9 p.636 #27 p.24 August 9, 1922 – #9 p.636 Pope Pius XI (April 1926) – #9 p.606; 636
Page 140	1926 (Orphanage) – #5 no. 129
Page 141:	Pope Pius XI (1928)– #9 p.607; 636
Page 142:	Pope Pius XI (1935) – #9 p.608; 636
Page 143:	Petitions to the Pope – #28 p.118; 119
Page 144:	Pope Pius XI (1937) – #9 p.605; 636 #27 p.24

Chapter 10

Page 146:	Pope Pius XI (1938) "Omnipotent Intercession" – #9 p.609; 636
Page 147:	Assumption of the Blessed Virgin Mother – #18 p.188 Pope Pius XII (1955) "St. Joseph the Worker" – #9 p.610 #27 p.24
Page 148:	Patronage of St. Joseph (1955) – #11
Page 150:	Pope Pius XII (1958) "Radio Broadcast to American School Children" – #9 p.616–618; 636

Chapter 11

Page 155:	Pope John XXIII (1959) – #9 p.619; 636 Fulton J. Sheen – Oratory, 1961
Page 157:	Pope John XXIII (1961) (Apostolic Letter) – #9 p.619–629; 636 #27 p.24
Page 167:	Pope John XXIII (1961) (Allocution) – #9 p.629–631; 636
Page 170:	Pope John XXIII (1962) – #3 p.104 #9 p.636
Page 171:	First International Symposium on St. Joseph – #22
Page 172:	Second International Symposium on St. Joseph – #23
Page 173:	Third International Symposium on St. Joseph – #24
Page 174:	Fourth International Symposium on St. Joseph – #25

Epilogue

Page 182:	Pope John-Paul II (Redemptoris Custos) – #12

INDEX

A

Agreda, Venerable Mary of 60
Ailly, Pierre d' 46
Albert the Great, St. 33
Alexis, Brother 56
Allen, Frances 74
Alphonsus Liguori, St. 69
Ambrose, St. 18, 21
America 50
André, Brother 78, 88, 92, 103, 120, 126, 129, 130, 138, 141, 144, 145, 170, 172, 173, 174, 176, 177
Anastasia, St. 20, 28
Apollonia 20
Aquinas, St. Thomas 34
Assumption of the Blessed Mother 147
Athanasius, St. 21
Augustine, St. 18, 25

B

Barat, St. Madeleine Sophie 78
Bede, Venerable 30
Benedict XIII, Pope 73, 99
Benedict XIV, Pope 74
Benedict XV, Pope 133, 138, 160
Bernard, St. 32, 70
Bernadette of Lourdes 92, 95, 127
Bernadine de Bustis 48
Bernardine of Loredo 52
Bernardine of Siena, St. 39
Bessette, Alfred: see André, Brother
Bolland, Jean de 60
Bonaventure, St. 34
Bonum Sane 133
Bossuet, Jacques-Benigne 62
Bourget, Bishop Ignace 81, 88, 92, 121, 126, 177
Bridget of Sweden, St. 38
Brindisi, St. Lawrence of 55
Butler, Alban 73

C

Callistus, St. 18
Cap-de-la-Madeleine 102
Carmelites 66, 68, 86
Catacombs 18
Charles II, Spain 67
China 73
Chrysologus, St. Peter 29

Chrysostom, St. John 18, 22
Clement X, Pope 67. 98
Clement XI, Pope 73, 98
Communism 144, 149
Constance, Council of 45
Cortona, St. Margaret of 37

D

Damascene, St. John 18
Damian, St. Peter 32
Dark Ages 30
Drexel, Blessed Katherine 119
Dujarie, Jacques 78, 79
Durocher, Bl. Marie-Rose 103, 120

E

Ephrem, St. 21
Epiphanius, St. 18
Europe 66
Eymard, St. Pierre Julian 79

F

Faber, William Frederick 84, 126
Fatima, Apparition of 131
Folk Literature 56
Francis de Sales 57, 68, 86
Frederic, Fr. 129
French Revolution 77

G

Gerson, John 45, 86
Gregory XV, Pope 66, 98
Grey Nuns 120, 126

H I

Hilary, St. 18
House of Loreto 35
Hupier, Fr. 122

Immaculate Conception of the Blessed Virgin 92
Inclytum Patriarcham 98
Inocent XI, Pope 68
Isolano, Isadore de 51

J

Jerome, St. 18, 27
Jesuits 86, 87
John of the Cross, St. 55
John Paul II, Pope 182
John XXIII, Pope 155, 157, 167, 170

Josaphat, Valley of 28
Joseph and Labor 133
Josephology 149
Joseph's Oratory, St. 120, 126, 129, 130, 138, 144, 145, 148, 150, 170, 173, 174
Joseph the Hymnographer, St. 31
Jugan, Jeane 82
Justin, St. 17, 19

K L

Kidron Valley 28
Knights of Columbus 138
Knock, Our Lady of 103

Lawrence of Brindisi, St. 55
Leonard of Port Maurice, St. 68
Leopold I of Austria 66
Leo XIII, Pope 99, 106, 107, 115, 118, 182
Lepicier, Alexis H.M. Cardinal 125
Little Sisters of the Poor 82
Loreto, Holy House of 35
Lourdes of Canada 120
Luther, Martin 51

M

Margaret of Cortona, St. 37
Mary Major, Rome 18
Mary of Agreda, Venerable 60
Mexico 50
Middle Ages 30, 47, 172
Miracle Staircase 100
Moreau, Fr. Basil 79, 81, 88

N O

Neminem Fugit 115
Newman, John Henry Cardinal 89
Notre Dame, Indiana 82

Origenes 17
Old St. Joseph's Church 73
Omnipotent Intercession 146

P Q

Patron of the Universal Church 22, 26, 32, 46, 96
Paul VI, Pope 173
Philadelphia, Old St. Joseph's 73
Pius IX, Pope 89, 92, 96, 98, 109, 117, 158
Pius X, Pope 107, 126, 127, 130, 159
Pius XI, Pope 138, 141, 142, 144, 146, 150, 161
Pius XII, Pope 147, 150, 161
Prayers & Devotions 213
Priscilla, St. 18
Provençal, Fr. André 120

Quamadmodum Deus 96
Quamquam Pluries 107, 117, 182

R

Raphael 49, 50
Real Estate 211
Redemptoris Custos 182
Reformation 51
Relics 28

S

Santa Fe, New Mexico 100
Schism, Great of 1054 31
Schism, Great of West 39
Schism, of East 48
Sheen, Bishop Fulton J. 155
Shrine 176
Sixtus IV, Pope 48, 98
Staircase 100
Suarez, Francisco 55
Symposium, Fifth International 210
Symposium, First International 171
Symposium, Fourth International 174
Symposium, Second International 172
Symposium, Third International 173

T U V

Tapestry 180
Teresa of Jesus, St. (Avila) 52, 86
Theresa of Lisieux, St. (Little Flower) 119
Thomas Aquinas, St. 34
Trent, Council of 55

Valley of Josaphat 28
Vaughan, Herbert Cardinal 92
Vitali, Canon Antonio 105
Voci, Le 157

W X Y Z

Westphalia, Peace of 60

d'Youville, St. Marguerite 120